ELIZABETH PÉLADEAU

1 Story
1 Message
1 Playlist

Distribution by Amazon KDP and Ingram Spark (P.O.D.)

Printed in the United States of America and Canada
Title: My Egregore
Author: Elizabeth Péladeau
Publisher: Talk+Tell
Typeset: Paul Neuviale
Cover designer: Charlotte Pearce
Photography: Pazit Perez

Hardcover ISBN: 978-1-7773916-5-2
Paperback ISBN: 978-1-7773916-4-5
eBook ISBN: 978-1-7773916-6-9

Legal Deposit: Bibliothèque et Archives nationales du Québec, 2022

Book description: A compelling and inspiring read that invites you to discover the culture, history and food of Elizabeth's native Quebec, *My Egregore* is an intimate look at what shapes our identity and the connections we treasure.

I dedicate this book to my family, my friends, and everybody who helped make up my egregore.

Contents

RECIPES

My goal with this book is to make you smile, maybe reflect, maybe even sing and dance a little!

EGREGORE

One day, I felt a great need to recharge my batteries, and I followed my sister to a yoga class. Our father had left us for another world, and our mother seemed to be following the same path. My heart was in pieces. I had already taken yoga classes here and there, but I had never encountered what I was about to experience.

After several stretches that made me discover muscles that I did not know I had, our teacher suggested that we take the position of the tailor for the Pranava meditation. She explained that we were going to do a chant often practiced by Buddhist monks: "Om," the sound at the foundation of all sounds, a vibration directly related to universal vibration. I listened, a little distracted. We all took our breath and started chanting, "Ommmmm..." And all of a sudden, the strangest thing happened. After a few seconds of chanting in unison with the others, I felt an incredible connection. We all felt it. (Yes, I know if you've never done this, it sounds a bit esoteric, but it is a common phenomenon in meditation and prayer.)

At that moment, I realized that we were all connected by a

bond of love, a special energy.

In my life, there were many happy coincidences and moments when I felt intensely connected to the people around me or who came before me.

I call this phenomenon my egregore.

It's an energy everyone of us has felt at some point, but never really knew how to describe. When describing such an energy, words tend to fail us. It feels special and intimate.

Egregores unite people with a common goal. Some companies have egregores, better known as their "culture." The same goes with professions, countries, communities, and families. Egregores can also be found in artistic expression.

Our relationship to various art forms and the emotions they elicit can give us hints about what defines us as an individual. When we have strong emotional reactions to art, we come into contact with an egregore. Sometimes, when someone writes a song, makes a movie, or paints a picture, they encapsulate their emotions in one piece, making it communicable to the person who looks at it or listens to it.

This connection doesn't happen every time we see a movie or listen to a song. It is reserved for those rare moments when it feels like a piece of art seems to almost get into our bloodstream and touches something deep inside of us. This happened to me when I saw the movie *Amistad* in 1997. My uncle, a big shot businessman, had been in a coma for three weeks. It felt weird to come to the realization that even such a strong man would some day die. *If he can die,* I thought, *anyone can die too.* I was going through a rough patch, and I went to the movies to escape. *Amistad* was so well done that I felt I was right there in that movie. And I truly felt that even if death comes to us all, we are never really alone. Through community and helping each other, we can be stronger, and we can make challenges easier to bear. Storytelling itself is a community-building tool.

Music is another good example. When a song brings back memories and connects us to powerful emotional states that give us chills, love, and strength, we are given a clue about what makes us who we are. It's not merely about listening to a song. It's about the way the song makes us feel, and the memories it brings back. Music is one of the most powerful tools to alter one's mood or relieve stress. Before people could read, music was the favoured medium for storytelling.

Music makes my heart beat and makes me travel elsewhere, from yesterday to today. It gives me freedom, invigorates my mind, and sometimes gives me solutions! Music is part of my history. My experiences, thoughts, dreams, emotions, adventures, everything in my life has a soundtrack to it. When I listen to a song, I am taken back in time or pushed forward into the future with hope and renewed motivation.

I have chosen to add a playlist of songs to every chapter of this book because music is always linked to my memories and my experiences. Just like in a movie, to enter and escape into my world, you will need my playlist to set the right tone. A QR code is available for you to listen to the playlists on Spotify, so you can be transported to the right time and place![1]

Music may very well be a part of your egregore as well. But really, your egregore is the sum total of your existence,

1. To access the QR codes, turn on your phone camera and put it over the code. A link will pop up, and you can access the playlists.

impressions, and encounters. It includes all the generational patterns you have inherited and perpetuated. It includes every single friend, enemy, lover, parental figure, child, mentor, mentee. This energy holds on to everything that has ever happened to you and every impression and emotion you have ever felt.

But it is as much about what you absorb as it is about what you put out. The way you change the energy in a room when you walk into it. The gratitude that a friend has when you comfort them. The values you teach to your children. The inspiring social media posts you shared with your loved ones. In its highest form, an egregore radiates love and engulfs the world around you.

If you have ever gotten a strong "vibe" coming off of another person, object, or place, something you couldn't quite put your finger on, then you have come into contact with this ever-present, ever-changing, free-flowing force.

We live our daily lives often repeating the same actions, the same routine, the same daily grind, taking a lot for granted. But do you sometimes stop and ask yourself the question, "Who am I?"?

Could you be the sum of the experiences of all your ancestors? Have you ever considered the extent to which you were strongly influenced by your experiences, your parents, and even your grandparents, the people you meet, the places you go, coincidences, and what you do with all of this? How do you interpret your history and that of the people who came before you?

I had a good childhood. It wasn't perfect, but I don't

believe in perfect. Perfect doesn't teach us anything. Perfect has no history. Perfect is boring. But I was lucky. Lucky to be surrounded by solid, authentic people who inspired me.

But my goal in this book is not to talk about myself, even if I will do that a lot. My goal is to inspire you, give you a little lift, a little boost to help you get through your day, and at the same time give you a little food for thought, by sharing a story, a message, and a playlist!

Every chapter ends with a section filled with prompts designed to help you ask yourself the right questions to connect and to get closer to what makes you you.

Maybe answering them will spark some new conversations, helping you discover your deeper self, your essence, your egregore, and the people you are lucky to have around you!

CHAPTER 1

MY ESSENCE

We don't receive wisdom; we must discover it for ourselves after a journey that no one can take for us or spare us.

—MARCEL PROUST

PLAYLIST

Who Are You · THE WHO
Memories · MAROON 5
Time · PINK FLOYD
Who Are You When I'm Not Looking · BLAKE SHELTON
Parle-moi d'toi · KAÏN
Think · ARETHA FRANKLIN
Pour un instant · HARMONIUM
Dégénérations · MES AÏEUX

Do you ever wonder who you are? Do you ever wonder what influences your life?

I remember being pregnant with my son. I was reading everything I could find, tracing every step of his growth. His ears were forming, his head, his heart… I wondered what kind of personality he would have, what colour of hair? Would he be like my husband or me? Would he have my mom's blue eyes?…

Months flew by. It was time to give birth. My stress went through the roof, and I felt the pressure of wanting to be a good parent, a perfect parent, guiding him to be the best he could be.

I wanted to be a good cook like my mom, a good entrepreneur like my dad; the list of all the great things I wanted to be went on and on. I realized with time that I could not be *everything*. It might be too late for me to be an astronaut. I had to take a good look at myself and find the right fit for me, the right fit for who I am, for what makes me unique, my essence. What does that mean?

I started a quest to find who I was, besides Jean and Gisèle's daughter, Martin's wife, and Charles's mother, because if I wanted to be the best version of me, I needed to know who "me" was. Even if you live with yourself everyday, it's easy to forget who the real you is. It's easy to forget your essence!

This journey I was taking required a little research and a lot of introspection, remembering the good old days before being a mom, before being an adult, even before existing! I needed to understand my history and where I came from before I could hope for anything in the present or in the future, for myself or even for the generation following me!

JEAN FROM FRANCE

I did a DNA test and I found out my ancestors are seventy-four percent from France, seven percent Italian, and a mix of Irish, Scottish, and Spanish (My last name, Péladeau, derives from the Spanish *pelado*), and a mish-mash of other things, even African!

Four hundred years ago, a big move established my foundation. A certain Jean is responsible for a big part of my destiny.

My ancestor Jean (who had the same name as my dad) came from Poitou, a province of west central France. We don't know much about him except that he lived to be a hundred years old, and he was a carpenter from Aulnay, a village bordered by a vast forest that stocked all the province in heating and construction wood. He probably attended Sunday church at Eglise Saint-Pierre, which today is a UNESCO World Heritage Site. He courageously took the boat on May 24, 1665, and he is the reason I am here today writing to you from Montreal. Some would rather tell you they are of royal descent; I sort of like the fact that my ancestors were courageous adventurers that crossed the ocean. I like to imagine their resilience in building a life for themselves very far away from anything they knew. This explains why I eat French food and why going to church on

Christmas is important to me (even if it is mainly for singing), which my ancestor Jean probably did. It might even explain why my father and my grandfather were lumber merchants.

I imagine many other secrets lie in my DNA. In a way, those secrets, hidden in the depths of time, are the embryo of my essence.

THE HOUSEHOLD GENERATION GAP

My first impulse when I think of who I am is to think of my parents. But besides their DNA, what else influenced them? I would be a very different person if my parents had been born ten years earlier or ten years later. They did have an age difference of eleven years—quite a gap. Being part of my generation had a great influence on my nature but having three different generations under the same roof every day for twenty years rubs off on you too.

My dad was part of the Greatest Generation—funny name. They were called that because they lived through the Great Depression and fought in the Second World War. They had common characteristics: solid beliefs in personal responsibility, financial prudence, integrity, work ethic, faithful commitment. This really described my father to a tee in business as in his personal life.

Mom shared some of those values but was part of the Silent Generation who were raised during a period of war and economic depression. They were categorized as thrifty, respectful, loyal, determined, and having traditional values and a sense of self-sacrifice. When my mom said her wedding vows, she had to promise to be obedient to her husband. As years went by, she told us how much she hated that. My mom never had a job after we were born. She always had dinner on the table and she was always present. I think self-sacrifice really describes her well. When I had a hole in my sock, she would mend it. We did not buy new shoes often because we would take them to the shoemaker, and they looked brand new when we picked them up. She said *vous* to her mom (a sign of formal respect in French). To me, that sounded crazy, but for my mom it was a due mark of respect for the woman who raised her. Yes, the Silent Generation really described my mom, but as decades went by, I think she found it more and more difficult to be silent!

My older sisters Carole and Josée are Generation Jones (from the expression "keeping up with the Joneses"), also called Baby Boomers 2. Their generation lived through the sexual revolution of the sixties and seventies, the new television era, the oil crisis, Watergate… They were described as the generation that rejected and redefined traditional values. The idea of war and economic depression were fading away, and now the neighbours started comparing lawns, and how much greener one was over the other.

But in our house, the biggest wave of change came from feminism. My sisters were from the same generation; they were very different, but they both agreed on one thing: women were men's equals at home and in society. You could say my father, being a minority in the house, was the one who was getting an education on the subject. Maybe it would explain why he was so open minded later in life (and I do stress, *later in life*).

Carole was the perfect image of revolution. She wanted my mom to be more liberal, to let dad cook the meals and do the dishes. She challenged the idea of marriage. She wore mini-skirts and embraced peace and love; it became an important topic for her throughout her life. My other sister Jo was in the same generation but did not care for the same topics as Carole. She loved animals, fashion, and like me, she loved TV (something the older generations did not grow up with). She did not like to follow any trends or anyone else, and she agreed with the idea of enjoying more freedom!

And later I came along with the influence of my cohort, Generation X, raised with minimum adult supervision, valuing independence and work-life balance, informality, technology, and flexibility. My sisters always complained that my parents were a lot less strict with me than they were with them. Yes, they were. It might be because I was the youngest child, but maybe it had something to do with our changing society.

And society was undergoing tremendous change! Both of my grandmothers were not allowed to vote until 1940 (the rest of Canadian women had enjoyed suffrage since 1925, but France would wait until 1944). In 1964, a law passed to say that women no longer needed their husbands to sign contracts on their behalf. In 1969, contraception was decriminalized. In 1981, Quebec women were allowed to keep their maiden name after marriage, which quickly became the norm. My eldest sister was the first one to keep her name. Later, I did the same thing. Why should I give up a name that defined me for all my life? You could say women's lib had a big impact on our family and on my essence!

A FIVE-YEAR OLD DETECTIVE

Okay, I was influenced by my DNA and my generation as well as those around me, but then my nature started to manifest.

I was five, maybe younger. We were sitting in the car, all three girls in the back with me in the middle, my father was driving and my mom was assisting. I was asking questions. I wanted to understand everything in life. I got on my sister's nerves with my zillion questions. After a negative comment from her, I was about to stop, but then my mother turned around and said, "Asking questions is a sign of intelligence!" What a great motivation to continue—*forever*. Being curious and asking questions is a strong part of my essence to this day.

On what might have been the same day or a similar one, we were all sitting in the car again. Being the youngest and an extrovert surrounded by introverts, I felt the need to talk, express myself, and tell stories, so I did quite a lot. Why not? I had an audience and they were not going anywhere! My father would joke, "Hey, do you need any oil for that jaw? All that talking, it must be exhausting!" So it was clear I had to communicate. I had to tell stories. That was more important to me than anything else. My true nature was communicating—through talking, writing, photography, video...

THE SIX-YEAR-OLD BUSINESS WOMAN

As the last of three girls, I gained the affectionate nickname La Puce ("the flea"). I was just a little kid depending on the "big" people. Sometimes, nobody thought I was listening or that I understood.

Remember, my father is from a generation in which women were homemakers. So naturally, he thought his daughters would turn out to be homemakers. That's just the way things were.

When I was six years old, I was walking to the car holding my dad's hand while he was talking to my mom. He said something along the lines of, "Be realistic Gisèle, Elizabeth will get married and become a housewife and a homemaker…" He was talking as though I wasn't even there, thinking that kids don't really listen when adults talk anyway.

But I felt incredibly insulted. I immediately let go of his hand and took my distance, crossing my arms and taking a haughty attitude.

"I'm going to be a business woman," I said with assurance. "Maybe I'll even buy your business!"

I gave him a just-watch-me kind of attitude, and then looked away to measure the effect of my delivery. That day, my essence had spoken through me. With that memory, I had a piece of the puzzle of my purpose in life.

As a child, I tended to be more in touch with my essence because I had not learned to repress my instincts yet. This happened later, when I started paying attention to what society told me about how I was *supposed* to behave. However, my early childhood instincts have a lot to teach me about who I was meant to be in this world.

TRANSITION TO ADULT LIFE

In the following years, I lost touch with my essence. Like most adolescents, I couldn't quite put my finger on what I wanted to do in life. I thought I wanted to be a diplomat for a while, so I studied politics. I enjoyed most of my classes but realized it was nothing like I had imagined.

At the time, I was also taking classes in marketing and management. In one class, our assignment was to have a debate. We were divided into groups of six and asked to come up with the best arguments in order to convince the rest of the class that we were right. My group was made up of introverts, so no one wanted to do any public speaking, and no one wanted to be a leader. But I really wanted to win this debate, so I ended up coaching everyone in the group, instilling in them my knack for public speaking and debating.

We ended up winning the debate. Everyone in the group had managed to surprise themselves and step up to the plate. I managed to build up everyone's confidence, and they all thanked me for it, because they succeeded in being the best version of themselves. I was really proud of myself for this, and I loved every minute of it. Furthermore, I loved my marketing classes. My future started to take form. It started to get clearer for me: I had to work in business!

This gave me another piece of the puzzle that is the enigma of my essence. I got yet another piece at my wedding, when my cousin gave a speech about how I saw life through rose-tinted glasses. It reflected my motto, "good vibes only"—that's my essence. No one finds their essence in a single climactic moment. We find a piece here and there, and eventually the pieces we have gathered will start to tell a story. Our story.

When I looked at my mom, the warmth that she brought to the home, and the joy that the family felt when we were sitting down for dinner, I knew that I wanted to have a family of my own some day. But when I looked at my dad, I knew I wanted to be an entrepreneur. When I met one of my mom's best friends' daughter who worked in marketing, I was inspired to start working in advertising, in magazines, and later as an entrepreneur and now an author!

My essence can be found in the people I looked up to throughout my life, and especially, in the reasons why I admired these people.

Getting in touch with your essence is about letting go of people's expectations of you, letting go of questions like, "What will they say? What will they think of me?"

Your essence is how you roll. The rules your heart sings to you. Sometimes you cannot hear the song loud and clear because you are listening to your head and all the crazy tornadoes rolling around in there wanting you to listen to *them* instead of *yourself.*

Sometimes you need to sit and listen to your heart, see what you have been missing, realize the luck you have had and the wonderful people who helped pave your way.

If your essence is your roots, growing deep inside the Earth, your egregore is the energy of your branches reaching to the sky, feeling the warmth of the sun.

I finally found my essence. I realized I could not be *everything* but I could be *me,* the best me that I could be. My essence is rooted deep inside me but it evolves every day, throughout my life. I am French, a Montrealer, a Quebecoise, a Canadian, a North American, a woman with strong values, a good mom, a good wife, a loyal friend, a family person, a creative, fun person, a good listener, a music lover, a chocolate lover, an animal lover, a good food lover, a dancer and a singer (bad but passionate), a storyteller, a communicator, a passionate woman with a strong sense of *joie de vivre*. It's my essence, my uniqueness.

My son will soon be twenty years old. He is tall, looks like his dad, and often acts like him. I also see a lot of myself in him. He has dark brown eyes like my dad. He is a great communicator, a great human being… He is a mish-mash of all of our big family, our DNA, our experiences, the influences of our generations…

I still want to guide him and tell him what to do but I have to come to the realization that he is an adult now. Time flies. I have to do the hardest thing a parent has to do: *letting go*. I have given him a very large toolbox, from the second I learned I was pregnant up until today.

Now my job is to be here when he needs me. I have to trust that he will listen to his heart, follow his calling, understand his essence, and live a few egregores along the way!

I hope my story, my essence, my egregore, help you get closer to yours.

PENNY FOR YOUR THOUGHTS

What's your story? What is your essence? What has influenced it? What is your motto? How has your generation influenced you? How did your parents influence you? Your friends? Your neighbourhood? What do you know about your DNA?

CHAPTER 2

MUSIC: MY WELL-BEING, MY DRUG, MY TIME MACHINE

Music gives a soul to our hearts and wings to our thoughts.

—PLATO

PLAYLIST

Sunday Best · SURFACES
You're Beautiful · JAMES BLUNT
The Prayer · CELINE DION AND ANDREA BOCELLI
Dancing Queen · ABBA
La dernière valse · MIREILLE MATHIEU
Neiges · ANDRÉ GAGNON
L'ouverture-éclair · ANDRÉ GAGNON
Ce n'est rien · JULIEN CLERC
Jump in the Line · HARRY BELAFONTE
Guantanamera · JOE DASSIN
Lessons in Love · LEVEL 42
Just an Illusion · IMAGINATION
Use the Force · JAMIROQUAI
Thank You · DIDO
Good Enough · DODGY
Close to You · CARPENTERS
Les comédiens · CHARLES AZNAVOUR
Music · MADONNA
Time to Say Goodbye · ANDREA BOCELLI AND SARAH BRIGHTMAN
La Bamba · RITCHIE VALENS

Music is constantly present in my life. When I wake up, when I go to bed, when I walk, when I run, when I drive, when I am alone, with one person or in a group, whether I am happy or unhappy, when I think of a memory from thirty years or one year ago, with my father, my mother, or my husband, in Montreal or Paris, music inhabits my life.

Whenever I hear "Les comédiens" by Charles Aznavour, I remember my mom being happy. Whenever I hear the Carpenters, I remember my sister and her friends singing in the kitchen. Whenever I hear the *Sliding Doors* soundtrack, I remember that feeling of new and young love, and how I fell in love with my husband. Whenever I hear "Just an Illusion" by Julia Zahra, I feel lucky or inspired, and I experience a flash of happiness. Whenever I hear the band Level 42, I remember being on a boat near a tropical beach, in the middle of the ocean, cutting through the water and feeling like I am flying.

If the last sense we experience when we die is hearing, I hope to be played music from my favourite playlist while being softly told, "I love you."

What about you? How would you describe your experience with music? Do you ever hear a song and know exactly where you were the first time you heard it, and all of a sudden, you travel to a different time and a certain well-being lives in you?

Music always or almost always played in our house. I have distant memories of a piece of furniture in the living room,

23

rather art deco, probably inherited from my grandmother. It must have dated from the thirties. At the end, on the right, there was the turntable on which my parents played records, and in the middle of it was the radio with two big black buttons that we turned to choose a station. This massive piece of furniture took up a good part of the living room. It was a far cry from the iPod! We played happy music. My parents loved Latin music; it spread joy in the house. When it wasn't Los Tres Amigos, it was Jean-Pierre Ferland, Belafonte, Dalida, Ginette Reno, Piaf, Brel… They each had their turn.

1970. Before falling asleep in the evening, I grabbed my favourite trinket, a music box shaped like a horseshoe with a small family of mice painted on it. I turned it upside down and cranked it. "Au clair de la lune" was playing, and I fell asleep, happy. This was the beginning of my adventure with music.

1975. I went to the dentist with Mom. He had a comforting last name: Dr. Lamoureux. In the waiting room, Mom picked up a magazine. The radio played on the speaker located in the ceiling above us. It was CJMS, Mom's favourite radio station. Julien Clerc was crooning. They called my name; it was my turn to see the doctor. The sound of the drill and the fear of long needles invaded me. Fortunately, Mom was there… And so was Julien.

I was ten years old. I drove around with my mother. I didn't like her favourite radio station, CJMS (an FM station), and she didn't like mine, CKGM (an AM station). She described my style of music as "bing-bang-boom." One day, she found a compromise. A new discovery. A pianist. Mom loved the piano. She made sure that her three daughters learned to play it. She wanted us to fine tune our ears. She wanted us to listen to classical music, but I was not interested. I prefered Elton John's pieces to Beethoven's. But I was in *her* car, and *she* was the one driving. I had no choice but to listen to this new discovery of hers. Plus, she seemed so enthusiastic about it that I didn't want to disappoint her. She put on the tape. To my surprise, I liked it. It was André Gagnon, a Quebecois artist known for fusing classical music and pop. He was the youngest of a large family of nineteen children and began playing the piano at the age of six. He played songs for my favourite children shows, so maybe that's where he first caught my ear. He had recorded in Abbey Road Studios, just like the Beatles. His album, *Neiges*, stayed on the top 10 of the American Billboard charts for twenty-four weeks. For several weeks when I boarded the white Mercury Monarch with its red upholstery, there was a sense of harmony in the car—peace and a little happiness between mother and daughter. A really good vibe!

As I got older, I learned to love mom's music. Together, we listened to Dassin, Bécaud, Aznavour... I cherished those moments so much that many years later, I named my son Charles, after Aznavour, in honour of the moments shared with Mom, in her car, at home, and at Aznavour's shows.

Getting in the car with Dad to run errands when family friends came over on Saturdays was among my favourite car trips because we would often stop at Pâtisserie de la Gascogne. When we opened the door, it smelled like heaven. The owners had emigrated from France and opened this bakery in 1957. Dad would get the baguette, cheese, foie gras, cheese straws, cake, and if I was lucky, I would get a

Carambar (caramel candy imported from France).

In the car with Dad, the tempo was different. Mom played male musicians and Dad played female ones. Dad didn't love my mom's music; he found it depressing. I think he was jealous. If he had seen the look on Mom's face at a Charles Aznavour concert, I can assure you that he would be! With Dad, it was Dalida, Mireille Mathieu, Nana Mouskouri (Dad used to tell me every time, "You know she speaks six languages?")... One day, he got a new tape. He was very proud. He felt very hip. He told himself that with a band like this he was sure to catch my attention. It was popular with kids my age. When you're a parent, you don't necessarily want people to think you're old school! On the spot, I didn't love it, but it did strike me as more modern than Mireille and Nana. He put down the windows, and to make me laugh, or maybe to embarrass me, he raised the volume of his music and greeted passers-by by singing along to his new discovery: Abba! Embarrassed, I recoiled in the back of my seat, hiding. But deep down, I liked to spend time driving with my father. When I saw him transform to the sound of music, his enthusiasm was contagious.

Time flies. I was thirty-three years old. My father was getting older, and so were the people around him. I was taking my father to the hospital every day. His little brother, aged seventy-two, was in a coma from which he would not wake up. We were both heartbroken. I drove looking straight ahead, trying to be strong, but I had ten thousand questions constantly spinning in my head: *Why him? Why do we live? Why do we die? Where do we go? Who decides?*... I took a quick look at Dad who looked completely broken. I wanted to comfort him, but I couldn't find the words. We were both in shock. His brother was larger than life. I couldn't imagine the sadness he was experiencing. In addition to losing a brother, it dawned on him that he would be the last survivor of a family of seven children. The atmosphere was heavy. I put on a CD from a new singer who was turning into an international success. His brand new album was our latest discovery. He started singing with his amazing voice. I felt a tiny bit better. The questions in my head seemed to stop. The heaviness lightened for a moment, as if there was hope, as if life was greater than us, as if death did not exist for the length of this song. We felt less alone. Thank you, Andrea Bocelli, for coming to our rescue. Every time I hear Bocelli I am transported back in time to a hard but beautiful moment with my father, bound in sadness, love, and music all at the same time.

I became a mom. Much of my time was spent as the chauffeur of a miniature passenger, sitting in his car seat behind me. My father had left us. Sadness invaded me while behind the wheel as I thought of him. Suddenly I heard my miniature passenger singing, "You're beautifuuuul," and my heart melted. He echoed James Blunt on the radio, and he knew and mumbled all the lyrics. I saw him in my rear-view mirror, smiling, happy. Our eyes crossed; it was magical. We sang together in pure happiness. Music is still my savior. I am still in the car, the passengers have changed, but I feel like they are still there, with their good vibes, very close to me through love and music.

When the summer ends, I am always a little sad. But when I walk outside, put on my music, and "Love Generation" by

Bob Sinclar comes on, my pace accelerates, I feel energized, I have a huge smile on my face. Something happens in my body, my brain, my soul, and it's summer all over again.

My favourite show is *Ted Lasso*. I am always amazed by how good the storyline is. And then the music comes on—Piaf, Queen, Sam Cooke, Wham, Surfaces—I get goose bumps. The music is the cherry on top, the icing on the cake. It takes me to my happy place.

In the winter of 2021, in the middle of the pandemic, things looked a little stale. The pandemic days seemed like they would never end, and the weather was cold. I needed fresh air. I needed to go somewhere. So my husband suggested we go on a car ride with our dog Kayla. We turned on the music, and the song "Sunday Best" by Surfaces came on. I looked at Kayla, who had her nose outside the window and her ears flapping in the wind, and she looked happy. I looked at my husband, who was smiling, and he looked happy too. I was singing, I felt finally free, because I had everything I needed: love, a great song, and the feeling that everything was going to be okay.

Whether I'm driving, walking, or cooking, I listen to music and I smile. I am transported back in time. You can take everything away from me, but don't take away my music!

Music has a big place in my life. It is the number-one tool I use to help me stay sane. I'm not alone. Even Einstein admitted the importance of music in his life when he said, "If I wasn't a physicist, I'd probably be a musician. I often think in music. I live my daydreams in music. I see my life in terms of music. I get most of my joy in the life of music." Who knows, maybe it was one of his secrets to tap into his greatness?

If the last of our senses to die out is hearing, there may be a reason: Music is full of life.

PENNY FOR YOUR THOUGHTS

Is there a concert you've been to where the music created a magical energy that you felt all around you? Do you have any practices to help you get into that state? Yoga, tai chi, chi gong, prayer, meditation? What is your fondest childhood memory from a time where you and your parents had a genuine feeling of happiness and higher love? Maybe during a holiday season or a birthday? What project do you remember working on with a group of friends or family, where you were working towards a common goal you felt intensely connected to? What lifts you up in life?

Think about what the soundtrack of your life would sound like. What songs bring you joy, lift you up, take you back to happy memories? What songs motivate you? What are the favourite songs of the people you care most about—your mom, your dad, your partner, your kids, your best friend? What song do you think reminds them of you? What song can you not help but get up and dance to? What's in your favourite playlist?

CHAPTER 3

THE POSTCARD

To love is not to look at each other, but to look together in the same direction.

—Antoine de Saint-Exupéry

PLAYLIST

That's Amore · DEAN MARTIN
Over the Rainbow · VERA LYNN
Mes jeunes années · CHARLES TRENET
Some Enchanted Evening · PERRY COMO
A Sentimental Journey · DORIS DAY
Voulez-vous danser grand-mère · NICOLE CHANLY
Maître Pierre · GEORGES GUÉTARY
Swinging on a Star · BING CROSBY
Beyond the Sea · BOBBY DARIN
In the Mood · GLENN MILLER
La mer · CHARLES TRENET

One day during the Covid-19 pandemic, I was looking through old boxes, and I came across an old postcard written from my dad to my mom. It was written before they got married, when my dad Jean had to leave Montreal for Arnprior, Ontario to take intensive courses that would help him to finally have his own lumber trading company one day.

I pictured him sitting in his room, writing to my mom, knowing he would not be able to hear her voice in the coming days.

August 30, 1949
Arnprior, Ontario

Dear Gisèle,

I am sending you a note because I will not be able to call you tonight or tomorrow. I am going to the forest for a few days. I don't have to tell you that I'm terribly bored and that I miss you a lot. The day of my departure seems unbearably far.

Until I see you again,

Jean

Finding this postcard made me realize that before they were my parents, before they were married, my mom and dad were two individuals who happened to meet and fall in love. I tried to take myself back to the time that postcard was written. I invite you to sit comfortably and travel back with me to 1949 in Montreal, Quebec.

It was a regular day in Montreal. These were the years of La Grande Noirceur (The Great Darkness). Maurice Duplessis was in power. A celibate lawyer, married to church and province, against casual clothing, against feminism and modernism, often described as rigid and dictatorial.

The radio chose our songs for us, and these days, Lucille Dumont came on a lot, as well as Perry Como's successful song, "Some Enchanted Evening," and a few of the Glenn Miller Orchestra's sixty-nine top 10 hits. (They had more top 10 hits than the Beatles, Elvis, and Drake!) Television had arrived in the United States, but not yet in Quebec, so we were nailed to the radio. If it wasn't for music, it was for the news or soap operas, religion or hockey. "Hockey Night in Canada," later a popular TV show, originated as a popular radio program launched in 1931.

We did not hear about too many miracles performed by the church but plenty by Maurice Richard, our Superman French Canadian player! Maurice Richard, the "Rocket" of the Canadiens hockey team, performed at the Montreal Forum. The owners, the players, the coaches, almost everyone was English-speaking, even though when the team started, they were all French. He was one of the few French Canadians on the team, making him a symbol, a hero for francophones.

It was thanks to these years that we owe the beginning of a patriotism towards our Montreal hockey team!

On Saturdays, people met up at the Beaubien, Impérial, or Loew's cinema. Women rushed to movies featuring handsome Yves Montand, Humphrey Bogart, Clark Gable, John Wayne, Fred Astaire, and Gregory Peck, while men dreamed of Michèle Morgan, Ava Gardner, Marilyn Monroe, and Simone Signoret. In the theatre, La Poune and Olivier Guimond made all of Quebec laugh.

A loaf of bread cost thirteen cents, the minimum wage was forty cents, and a house cost an average of seven thousand dollars. Brand new that year were the 45 vinyl record and the Polaroid camera. (Taking a selfie was a lot more complicated back then!)

People smoked cigarettes because it was elegant; no one was talking about their harmful side effects yet. People drank Caribou (whiskey and maple syrup), gin, martinis, and Labatt beer. For children it was spruce beer or Crush cream soda.

Travelling was very uncommon. People were sedentary and didn't get too much influence from the outside world— yet! On your plate, you would find simple meals: pâté chinois (the Quebecois take on shepherd's pie), stew, or spaghetti... French cuisine influenced us day by day, and American food too. Since the end of the war, Jell-O was more popular than ever, making aspic a fashionable dish.[2] We found them in every shape, colours, and flavours.

Aspics were a must-have for every party, visually pleasing next to the eggs with mayo, pasta salad with mayo, ham with

2. See Recipes: Aspic (p. 222)

mayo, and small sandwiches cut into a triangle. (Kraft marketed its mayonnaise in 1930.) Unfortunately, diverse gastronomy from the world's farthest reaches was not yet accessible to the average Quebecois. In the French Canadian circles of Montreal, the influence was a beautiful mixture of French and English. Fast food had yet to catch on as a trend and mothers spent a lot of time in the kitchens. They had large families to feed, and meal times were seen as sacred.

We paid for things in cash, because no one owned a debit or credit card. Sometimes, we opened a tab to pay later, because everyone trusted each other. The word of a man had value, because we did not want to sin and have to confess it to the priest! After surviving through the war and the Great Depression, people saw wastefulness as a sin. A family of ten children was common, and the household finances had to be stretched so that the clothes of the first-born could make their way to the youngest. A garment was usually made in Quebec or simply made by Mom. Mothers spent a lot of time sewing, patching, cooking, and cleaning. They didn't really have time for themselves or for anything else!

Almost everything was made in Canada or not far away. The furniture was sturdy, made to last a lifetime, and would often be passed on to the next generation. Planned obsolescence was unheard of.

Women were elegant, rarely wearing trousers. Running shoes and blue jeans practically did not exist in town. Duplessis, the strict premier of Quebec, would not allow them!

At home, women often found themselves in the kitchen to work and men in the living room to relax! Kitchens were hidden away in a corner of the house, and no one had ever heard of an open-concept kitchen.

A man had to appear strong, never cry, and never talk about his feelings; otherwise, he could be seen as weak. So good communication in a marriage or at the office was rare. Marriage had to last a lifetime, whether you were with the right person or not. You made a promise, and you had to keep it.

Women had only been able to vote since 1940. The Catholic religion was very present in Quebec, a suffocating presence in fact, especially for the female gender. The families were large, thanks to the visits of the parish priests who repeated that a woman would go to hell if she did not do her duty to populate Quebec. Women stayed at home to look after children and men went to work. School had only been compulsory since 1943. This did not prevent some children from leaving school at the age of fourteen to help their parents. Divorces did not exist and neither did abortions. We didn't talk about homosexuality. We didn't smile in the pictures, and we didn't cry. Respect was the order of the day; authority was never put into question. Good communication didn't matter: the priority was to listen! At school, young women were taught to be good wives, good mothers, and good cooks.

Now you have a good idea of life in post-war Quebec. If you are from Quebec, then these are your foundations too, and they can explain the behaviour of many people and institutions to this day.

Nothing is truer than what Shakespeare said about the times we live in, "Know thou this, that men are as the time is."

This backdrop certainly explains a lot about Jean and Gisèle.

JEAN

1918. The end of the war. In Montreal, which Mark Twain called the city of a hundred bell towers, religion was everywhere, even in the names of children, because most children's names were picked out from the Bible. Jean, the fifth of a family of seven, was born that year.

Not overly religious, Jean still attended church most Sundays and every Christmas Eve. Like his father before him, Jean would also spend weekends in silent meditation with the Trappist monks at Oka Abbey, bringing back cheese and chocolate to be forgiven by his family for being absent for two days, and his family would devour everything. He didn't preach the words of the Bible, far from it, but he still remembered the important parts. He was honest, authentic, and generous, though impulsive and sometimes short tempered. Aware that he was not perfect, he did his best to always work on himself. All his life, he questioned the mystery of life and death.

With good reason. He was only seventeen years old when his father Henri died. An entrepreneur and avant-garde lumber merchant in the twenties, Henri imported machinery from Germany and travelled there often, at a time when people in Quebec travelled very little. He was very successful. He had a beautiful house in Outremont, a wife, seven children, a driver, and a cook... Life was beautiful until the day he trusted the wrong friends in business.

Unfortunately, this would teach him a lesson that would cost him his life and fortune: There are no friends in business. Henri had a word of honour, but unfortunately, not all men inherited the same righteousness as he did. At that time, a man's word was his bond—as binding as a legal contract. But again, not everyone followed this code of ethics.

When he decided to sell his services to make the most out of his new German machine (which was used to dry wood), some of his business friends said they were on board to pay him for these services. But with the looming Great Depression, they all bowed out, one by one. This caused a huge financial problem for Henri. First, he had to sell the machine, and then he had to sell his company. He went from being able to amply provide for his family to an everyday financial struggle. The loss of status and affluence was a blow for the whole family. The blow was so violent for Henri that he was struck by throat cancer and died at the age of fifty-one. When his children had to be pallbearers at his funeral, one of them had to get a winter coat from the Salvation Army.

Jean learned at a young age that when you have fortune and health everyone is there, but when you lose your fortune, there are often few people left. Only your true friends will stay. Loss and misfortune is a test of true friendship. This lesson was the hardest he ever had to learn, but it shaped his values, his character, and his family, guiding and motivating him.

After the death of his father, Jean developed a strong sense of responsibility towards his loved ones. He often found himself defending his three brothers, Henri-Paul, Jacques, and Pierre. His little brother Pierre called him "the lion of the family." He would retain this trait from childhood to old age, in different ways at different times in life.

One of Jean's younger brothers was a target of bullying

and Jean would often come to his rescue, getting himself in trouble. One time when Jean went to a camp run by priests with his other younger brother, Jean found him hiding behind a tree and asked him why. His brother explained that he was being mistreated by the priests. So Jean took him and left the camp, hitch-hiking all the way home. His mother thought Jean was lying, and it just confirmed her judgement of him: Jean was a troublemaker.

His mother was a strong, intelligent woman, very ahead of her time. She was the first in her community to obtain her driver's licence, and she made money on the stock market. But she could also be harsh, especially with Jean. She always doted on Jean's older brother who was a clean-cut scholar and a perfect child. She was a cultured, brilliant, intelligent woman, and Jean's older brother was her idea of what a son should be. But Jean wanted to follow in his father's footsteps in the lumber business, which didn't suit his mother's aspirations to intellectual, high-cultured pursuits. Jean was his mother's least favourite child, but probably his father's favourite.

What was important for Jean was to avenge his father. After the death of the latter, Jean would have different jobs, some of which would pay well, but none of which were particularly glamorous. So, while young boys his age were busy spending money, living their adolescence, and going out to bars, Jean prepared his revenge plan by keeping all his money in savings.

When his friends from the upper-middle-class neighbourhood of Outremont went out, they would take a cab paid for by their parents' money. Jean couldn't afford it, and he would pretend he had an errand to run along the way and would meet them later. And he would walk all the way to meet his friends. Throughout the whole walk, Jean would think, "One day, just watch me, I'll have the best car."

At the age of twenty-one, Jean enrolled in the army and spent three years in England. The environment was harsh, and he often saw his friends return from the front disfigured, amputated, or dead. He enlisted in the army with his best friend, a neighbour. One evening when Jean was on a forty-eight-hour leave, they made an appointment. Since a soldier is never late, when his friend got delayed, Jean knew that the next day, he would be the one to inform the family that his friend was missing in action. Another hard blow for Jean. During his life, he made many friends, but never shared a bond as strong as with this best friend.

In the evening, Jean would take the opportunity to study accounting and the lumber business. The Brits were fond of our young Canadians. Jean got invited to family homes, where he was fed fish and chips and plum pudding. He wasn't a huge fan of the latter but he was polite and always finished his plate with great effort. The patriarch of the family, thinking that Jean loved the food, asked his wife to serve him another helping. After his return to Montreal, Jean would refuse to eat plum pudding, no matter how good, until the end of his days.

After a three-year absence, he returned to Montreal. The return was difficult. He found a job in one of the largest timber companies in Montreal. He rose through the ranks, becoming vice-president. He worked hard and saved more money. He went out with friends and met some young women. But deep down, he had only one thing in mind: to become a lumber merchant and to rebuild his father's honour. Really, it's all he ever thought about.

One evening, a lady friend of his organized a fashion show. He went to greet her and met a young woman who worked for her, her niece Gisèle. He found her beautiful and charming. It was love at first sight and their lives were about to change…

GISÈLE

Gisèle was born in 1929, the year of the stock market crash and the beginning of the Great Depression. She was the eldest of ten children and was used to being in a house with an abundant family, a lot of life, and a lot of responsibilities. In many large families, the eldest often serves as a second mother. Gisèle was no exception. Her siblings considered her bossy, which is a normal trait for the eldest to have. Having more authority over the younger siblings, the eldest often takes on the role of surrogate parent and natural leader.

Cooking was considered an important part of homemaking. Family meals were a sacred time, and a woman's duty was to prepare comfort food for a large family. A lot of time was spent in the kitchen. Gisèle loved her siblings, but changing diapers and picking up after them didn't fulfill her passions. At seventeen years old, she needed adventure, she had a taste for freedom and life! She learned the right etiquette at school— cooking and homemaking. What she really wanted was to become a fashion designer like her aunt Jeannette, whom she admired. Lucky for her, Jeannette hired her and taught her the trade, while keeping her under her roof and charging her rent.

Gisèle was stylish, classic yet fashionable, always in a dress with a small-heeled shoe. Her red lipstick brought out her enchanting smile, pink cheekbones, and light blue eyes.

She loved music and film. She listened to Bing Crosby, Perry Como, and Charles Trenet, and often sang and danced in her room. She loved going to the Beaubien cinema to see the latest films with Gabin or Montand. War was still fresh in people's memories, so many young girls dreamed of a man in uniform, and Gisèle was one of them. At nineteen years old, she met Jean, an ex-army officer and a gentleman eleven years her senior! That would make a lot of people talk!

Jean and Gisèle had their first date at a café, then one at the cinema, and so on for a few weeks, months, and years. Gisèle often arrived late, sometimes by an hour! She was not very good at managing her time or the tramway system! Jean waited for her every time. He worried about his sweetheart. The idea of delays didn't go over well for a former army sergeant. Jean was never late. Once, to make a change, he decided to make *her* wait an hour. She learned her lesson and would avoid any delay—at least for a few months! Jean would get used to waiting for her in his car before each trip they took; he would learn to take that time for himself.

Jean was not patient or gentle, but Gisèle managed to appease him. Was it her *joie de vivre*, her smile, or her enchanting blue eyes that bewitched him? Probably a good mix of all three!

It didn't take long before Gisèle fell in love with Jean and Jean with Gisèle. But Jean was still busy with the idea of avenging his father. So he worked in lumber during the day and took long-distance courses on accounting and lumber in the evenings. That's when the postcard I found was written.

Gisèle's mother saw Jean as an old bachelor, uninterested in marriage, and advised her daughter not to wait and to find another party. But the truth was, Jean did imagine a future with Gisèle. But his mother would rather pair him off with a young neighbour from the upscale Outremont neighbourhood, a girl who came from a good family. Gisèle's modest background didn't suit Jean's mother. When Jean met the woman his mother wanted him to court, he found her nice, but the chemistry just wasn't there. It was with Gisèle that he wished to be, whatever his mother may have thought. He was looking for a true, authentic woman who would love him for who he was. And Gisèle was that person.

Gisèle was right to wait. On December 21, 1956, Jean and Gisèle married in secret with only two witnesses. A few months later, their first daughter was born.

They bought their first house, and when the family grew, they moved into a second one. Gisèle was responsible for everyone's well-being at home. She excelled at it, but spent a lot of time doubting herself, because the world had changed since her youth. Society did not value housewives as much as it used to. The liberation of women was gaining ground, and women were increasingly leaving the family nest to go to work. For a man of Jean's generation, allowing one's wife to work was frowned upon, as this would mean that the husband was not strong enough to provide for his family. He would be seen as weak. Gisèle would devote herself to her family like many women of her generation, but she would always have a little doubt, a little questioning… *What if?…*

Jean and Gisèle raised their children, their greatest happiness. Their second greatest happiness was entertaining their friends, sharing a good meal, washed down with a little alcohol, but most importantly with a lot of laughter, love, and real-life stories. Solid and generous, they supported many during divorces, bereavements, the good and bad surprises of life. Jean accomplished himself through his company, and Gisèle through the kitchen, pottery, bridge, dinner parties, and her family.

They got through the Quiet Revolution, the liberation of women, the technological revolution, they survived the crises of the seven, twelve, and twenty years of marriage. They transformed themselves through all stages of life. You are very different at twenty than at forty, fifty, or eighty!

Many years later, she was seventy-four years old, and he was eighty-five. They played golf and bridge together. Gisèle cooked his meals every day of their lives together. They had been married for almost fifty years. They were grandparents three times. They had travelled all over the world. They went through great joys and great sorrows, weddings and funerals. They mourned together the loss of close family and good friends.

They loved each other a lot even when communication occasionally broke down. During difficult times, they remembered those first moments. Their base, their foundations, their dreams. The family and human values they shared.

They went from young adults, to newlyweds, to young parents, to grandparents, to frail old humans. Life goes by fast.

Life is not perfect. A marriage is not always a nice walk in the park. When Jean and Gisèle got married, it was for better and for worse. We go through storms over fifty years, but we must cling to the beauty. And beauty, there was.

Sometimes a few words on an old postcard found in an old box remind us that before a pandemic, before a new great-grandson was born, before three adult grandsons, three daughters, and two elderly parents, there was a love story.

We tend to think very little about who our parents were before being "Mom and Dad," before they were married, before they had kids. That's something I often forgot when I was growing up. When we live in the moment, we don't think about how we will be perceived in ten, twenty, thirty years. Finding this old postcard made me realize how fleeting time is. I wonder if some day, my son will find an old letter I wrote before he was born, and find himself travelling back in time, to see the world through my eyes.

PENNY FOR YOUR THOUGHTS

Do you ever wonder about the influence of the times in your life? The society you were born in? The one you grew up in? The things you did when you were a kid that kids couldn't do today? How was your education different from your parents'? What do you think their mindset was when they were your age?

Do you know what kind of people your parents were before they had you? What were they like when they were kids? How did they meet?

CHAPTER 4

YOU CAN'T ALWAYS GET WHAT YOU WANT

Happiness is not about having what you want but about wanting what you have.

—CONFUCIUS

PLAYLIST

You Can't Always Get What You Want · ROLLING STONES
Father and Son · YUSUF CAT STEVENS
Daughters · JOHN MAYER
Maintenant je sais · JEAN GABIN

Have you ever wanted something so intensely and dreamed of it to the point of not seeing how lucky you were? While you think about it, here's a nice example.

My father was an entrepreneur, a lumber merchant. He was born on November 26, 1918, at a time when men dreamed of a son to perpetuate their name and their legacy.

My father was no different; he dreamed of having a son who would one day take over Bois Péladeau, the company he worked really hard on, with great passion.

One day, my mother was visiting her doctor. She was gaining weight; her hormones were playing tricks on her. Unfortunately, there were no home pregnancy tests at the time, so she went to the doctor who examined her in a rush and told her she was pregnant.

Everyone was very excited. My father worked hard at the office, happy at the possibility of finally having his son. He bought a new house because the last one was not big enough for the growing family.

As the months passed, my mother went back to the doctor for her follow-up pregnancy appointment. This time, he told her that she was not actually pregnant, and that he had gotten it wrong. Instead, she actually had a dangerously large fibroid which urgently needed to be operated on. He added, matter-of-factly, that she would never be able to have another child, hardly looking at her and using a cold and arrogant tone that didn't show a trace of empathy.

My mother was devastated. My father, furious.

My father had to mourn while worrying about my mother's health, not to mention the stress related to buying a new house. It was inconceivable to him that a doctor should make such a mistake. He found it negligent and inhumane. "If I ever meet him…" my father would rage.

Well it turns out that life is full of surprises, because he did happen to meet him one day, when my parents were invited to a cocktail party at a friend's house. They were shaking hands with people as they showed up, as you do. By chance, the infamous doctor appeared before my father, spreading his title at length before his name. Needless to say, when Dad heard his name while shaking his hand, he looked up at him, straight in the eyes. All it took was this damning look, and the poor doctor was afraid for his life. My mother had to get my father out of the cocktail party very quickly, because she too was afraid for the doctor's life!

Anger is the second stage of grief. And my father happened to be right in the middle of that stage when he coincidentally ran into the unfortunate doctor. My father was triggered, because he saw the perfect person to blame for what had happened. My dad's grief was particularly hard to overcome. He wanted a son so much because men were seen as protectors. And if he was gone, he was afraid there would be no one to take care of his wife and daughters. He also wanted someone to carry on the family name. At that time, a woman keeping her maiden name after marriage was unheard of. Today, as a tribute to my dad, I passed on his name to my son. Eventually, my mother managed to calm my father down, and they took comfort by telling themselves that they were very lucky to have two beautiful, healthy daughters.

Life goes on. Mom organized a garage sale, and to help her through her grief, she sold everything that could remind her of the coming of a baby.

Since life is full of twists and turns, the weeks passed, and one day, my mother learned that despite the fact that she had been told that she would never have any more children, she was pregnant, and this beautiful baby (me) was going to show up for the spring!

It turned out they were getting a third daughter, not the son my father was hoping for. Poor Dad. As the Rolling Stones sing, "You can't always get what you want, but if you try sometimes, you might find you get what you need." Maybe my father didn't need one boy but three girls!

Since my parents thought they would never have another child, my father realized it didn't matter whether he had a boy or a girl. Just having another child at all was fantastic news. Later, he would dote on all our boyfriends, and we had to make sure he liked them.

Why am I telling you all this?

Maybe because as I am writing this we are going through a pandemic, and it makes me realize that, when I stop to think about it, I have everything I need. Of course, part of me thinks I need more clients, more contracts, more trips. I would like to see my friends and family, but maybe right now, like many, I need to realize how lucky I am with what I already have.

Still, for a good part of my life, I was always looking

forward to something in the future: studying in Boston because it would be more exciting (never happened), my second child (who never came), the big New Year's Eve party (which is often a bit of a disappointment)…

I've heard so many times, "I can't wait for my vacation!" or "I can't wait to retire." It's as if we are always living in the future. What if this whole crisis that we are going through is meant to teach us to be more connected, more conscious, to live in the present moment, because we never know what awaits us?

I am a dreamer, an idealist. I often want more, but I realize that my happiest, most precious moments are not always accompanied by great music and fireworks.

When I think of the most beautiful moments of my life, strangely, they are small, simple moments.

The time my four-year-old son brought me my Mother's Day gift to bed: a beautiful plastic bracelet he made at the daycare, which I still have.

Every month of May, when I celebrate my birthday surrounded by my childhood friends, I stop for a moment to observe each of them to remind myself of how much I love them.

When I am with my family, my sisters, my nephews, my husband, my son, and we play Queen of Spades and my sister Carole tries to win (and fails!) and we burst out laughing!

When Friday pizza night comes, and I sit on the sofa by the fire with my husband, sipping our gin and tonics that he prepares for us with love, while he plays with my hair as we watch a good movie or a new series.

When my six-feet-tall, nineteen-year-old son tells me, "Good night, I love you," in the evenings before going to bed.

When I walk with my dog every morning, and she turns to me as if to say, "Have you seen how beautiful it is around us?"

Sometimes time passes, and you realize that what you wanted intensely may not have been what you needed.

My father had always dreamed of having a son, but life did things differently and instead gave him three daughters he adored, and finally a few years later, three grandsons of whom he was very proud.

Happiness is not found in the future but in the present moments of everyday life. Every day, you can find small jewels if you open your eyes wide enough.

It turns out that the Rolling Stones were right: You can't always get what you want, but you might find you get what you need. Thanks Mick!

PENNY FOR YOUR THOUGHTS

Was there a time in your life when you didn't get what you wanted and later found out that it was actually for the best? What are you grateful for? Do you feel you live in the present, or do you live for the future, thinking about when you will be rich, when you have your vacation…?

CHAPTER 5

ROSE: THE STRENGTH OF A MOTHER

A mother's love for her child is like nothing else in the world. It knows no law, no pity. It dares all things and crushes down remorselessly all that stands in its path.

—AGATHA CHRISTIE

PLAYLIST

What a Wonderful World · LOUIS ARMSTRONG
Lady Marmalade · NANETTE WORKMAN
La manic · GEORGES DOR
C'est beau la vie · JEAN FERRAT
Gigi l'amoroso · DALIDA
La ballade des gens heureux · GÉRARD LENORMAN
L'Amérique · JOE DASSIN
Pardonne-moi ce caprice d'enfant · MIREILLE MATHIEU
Soleil soleil · NANA MOUSKOURI
Le métèque · GEORGES MOUSTAKI
La prison de Londres · LOUISE FORESTIER
Je reviendrai à Montréal · ROBERT CHARLEBOIS
Un ange gardien · BEAU DOMMAGE
La complainte du phoque en Alaska · BEAU DOMMAGE
Le téléphone pleure · CLAUDE FRANÇOIS
Un éléphant sur mon balcon · ROGER WHITTAKER
Maman la plus belle du monde · LUIS MARIANO

1974. I was still a little girl. It was Mother's Day Sunday. We were heading to Mom's parents' house in Duvernay. Along the way, the radio played "Un ange gardien" by Beau Dommage ("A Guardian Angel").

I couldn't wait to see my cousins. As I mentioned before, Mom was the eldest of ten children, which meant that when the family got together, it was always a big party.

We were welcomed at the door as we arrived. Someone shouted, "It's Gisèle and Jean!" We came in and headed to Viviane's bedroom to put our coats on the bed, on top of a huge pile of clothes. Viviane was Mom's youngest sibling. My sisters went to meet cousins their age. Dad went to chat with the uncles, and Mom headed towards my aunts. I found Loulou, Isa, and Sylvie. The house was not big, and with ten siblings and their spouses and children, it was overflowing. We ran, we laughed, and we were quickly told to go play outside. On our way out, we got a small gift from Grandma: Crush cream soda. She always had them ready for us. This was our treat. Especially for me, because Mom never bought soda or junk food. Mom was very healthy and prefered to feed us brown bread and carrot juice. I heard her exclaim, "No, Mom!" but she wouldn't win. Everyone already had their bottle in hand and our grandmother replied, "It's only one soda!"

We drank in the small living room. The little ones came to join us to ask what we were playing. We hesitated to answer, because we didn't necessarily want to include them in the next game. At two or three years younger than us, we found them too young. To us, it seemed like a huge age difference. Finally, we invited them, because after all, the more the merrier. We ran outside to play hide and seek. The goal was to get to the back of a tree without being seen. Loulou covered her eyes and started counting. We ran in all directions. I hid behind a car. She passed by me. I wanted to laugh but I held back and started running to hit the goal. Phew! I was out of harm's way. We really had a lot of fun. We decided to play tag next.

The hours passed. A voice could be heard shouting, "Children, come and eat!" Famished, we rushed into the dining room to eat small triangle sandwiches, macaroni salad, celery with Cheez Whiz, sausages, stuffed eggs… The atmosphere was quiet for a few minutes.

We could hear the echoing voices of the adults. Uncle Claude told stories of his youth, but he was interrupted by his brothers Yvon and Gaston who corrected him. Everyone laughed. The music started playing, and the women started dancing.

Mom didn't see her siblings often, but I could feel she was close to them, happy to be in her world. I saw her in a different light. That night she was no longer Mom or Jean's wife, but the big sister, Georges and Rose's daughter. She was a Guy (her maiden name).

The adults finished eating dessert and made way for coffee and digestifs. We slipped away further into the house. Uncle Paul came to see us. He had gray hair and beautiful blue eyes. He told us jokes, left us for a few seconds, and then came back to tell us the same jokes. We laughed and pretended that this was the first time we heard his joke. I pretended to laugh, but really, it made me incredibly sad.

Uncle Paul lived with my grandparents. As a twenty-one year old accounting student, he became engaged. He was madly in love and had a whole future ahead of him. Everyone was so proud of him. He had it all—looks, intelligence, love. One evening, he went out with some friends, and they collided head on with a big truck. His friend sitting in the front passenger seat died instantly. The driver survived with only broken ribs, and Uncle Paul, who was in the back, survived but with a head injury. He lost his short- and middle-term memory, remembering his childhood but forgetting what he did in the last few minutes.

At the hospital, his fiancée visited him every day, and each time, he asked her who she was. She came back hopeful, until one day she stopped coming. Uncle Paul lost his fiancée, his job, his career, his future. He went back to live with my grandparents. He had a whole support system to help him, with his parents at the helm.

My grandmother was put under a lot of pressure to get him into an institution. It was a huge source of stress for her, but she didn't want to hear it; he was *her* son.

When Paul was in the hospital, he no longer walked, no longer spoke, and was labeled "vegetative." Every day, my grandmother was there. Having no car or driver's licence, she travelled two hours by bus to be by his side. In the fifties, if a child had any intellectual disability, they were automatically put in a psychiatric hospital, no questions asked. The doctor was firm with my grandmother. He had "managed" to find Paul a place at Hôpital Saint-Jean de Dieu, a psychiatric asylum. The ambulance was supposed to take him away, but Rose kidnapped him and took him home without telling her husband. She had made her decision. There was no discussion to be had. She was a woman of principle, and one of those principles was that she would never let one of her children down. She put everything in place to ensure an almost normal life for Paul.

Paul was not the first child Rose had to care for into adulthood. She did the same thing for her daughter Viviane, born with a learning disability, and kept her home against doctors' recommendations. She taught her how to be independent despite her challenges. Eventually, Viviane found love, work, and a place to stay.

When Rose passed away, everyone was very worried about my grandfather, about Viviane, but especially about Paul. There were some challenges, but they did well. Every morning they left for their health walks. When my grandfather passed away, Uncle Paul became a little more lost. He lived with one of my uncles. Eventually, he ended up in the hospital. Mom went to visit him, and every time, she came back distraught. Between the four walls, without the love of my grandparents, their stimulations and routines, he died. First mentally and then physically.

Love is a strong medicine. It's unequivocal. It can prolong a person's life and quality of life. It can save a life!

I didn't know much about my grandmother. When I saw her, she was a little harsh and sometimes called me Carole,

Josée, Sylvie, but rarely by my name, Elizabeth. I didn't blame her. I understood very well that with ten children and almost twenty grandchildren, my name was lost in the balance. With all these people around her, she rarely had the time or the inclination to chat. So, I knew her by learning from her actions and through my mother. When I saw her, she looked small, frail, and fragile. But the things that matter most are often invisible to the naked eye. I didn't see the extreme strength of this little woman. I didn't realize the value of the challenges she had to overcome.

When misfortune strikes, we try to find the reason, the meaning behind it. Lessons are not always immediately obvious. Sometimes the lesson is greater than us. We can only see it in hindsight. And the insight can take a generation to make itself known.

My grandparents didn't have an easy life: raising a family of ten children, two of them with disabilities, and the stress of almost losing a son. Despite this, I have never heard them complain.

Being a parent means that one day we will have to separate from our children. It can break our hearts to see them leave home and be independent, but it is a necessary part of life. We can see it as a new chapter where we have the opportunity to rediscover ourselves.

Rose and Georges made a huge sacrifice by keeping two children at home, but their ten children and grandchildren were given an incredible lesson.

I am convinced that this trait of human character made my father fall in love with my mother. She had a relentlessly humane side to her. She didn't judge. She was authentic and true. She was always looking at the good side of people.

I am aware that through my DNA I have inherited several traits from several families and that it is not possible to be sure about who transmitted what to me. Despite this, I like to believe that in me there is a little bit of Rose and Georges, a strength, solid values that remind me that against all odds and despite all external pressures, we do everything for those we love.

There are plenty of people like my grandparents, but they don't make the headlines; they don't seek attention or cameras. They are true and authentic, and have no interest in flash or glory. These people are jewels. Sometimes you just need to dig a little deeper to find the hidden treasure.

PENNY FOR YOUR THOUGHTS

Is there someone you know who has amazing strength and a story of resilience? Did you ever get the wrong idea about them? Maybe you thought they were cold and distant, but later you found out that the way they showed their love was through their actions, rather than through an obvious display of affection?

CHAPTER 6

HOME IS WHERE THE HEART IS

The house is the starting point of hope, love and dreams.

—Anonymous

PLAYLIST

Home to You · SIGRID
Our House · MADNESS
Je reviens chez nous · JEAN-PIERRE FERLAND
Ma main a besoin de ta main · CHARLES AZNAVOUR
Plus tôt · ALEXANDRA STRÉLISKI
To Build a Home · THE CINEMATIC ORCHESTRA
Take Me Home, Country Roads · JOHN DENVER
Home · PHILLIP PHILLIPS
Home · MICHAEL BUBLÉ
Home · EDWARD SHARPE & THE MAGNETIC ZEROS
Close to You · CARPENTERS
What a Wonderful World · LOUIS ARMSTRONG
La maison où j'ai grandi · FRANÇOISE HARDY

May 10, 2003, 3:00 p.m. The moving truck was turning the corner. I was coming back into the house to say a final goodbye. This was my last time in this house. I was heartbroken. I felt like I was losing a family member.

I was invaded by stories, memories, flashbacks…

THE PURCHASE: IT'S A START

1963. Dad learned that his family was growing. He wanted more space. He started looking. He met up with a neighbour, his childhood friend, André. André was a real estate agent who lived next door to Jean's house in Outremont when they were young. The two became life-long friends. André urged Jean to come and see this cottage. The lady who lived there, Mrs. Paradis, was a widow and wanted to sell. The cottage ran along the edge of the water. Mrs. Paradis lived there for many years with her family, but her life had taken another turn.

It was a country house with two doors: the front door was mostly used for guests and for Dad, and the side door led into a laundry room area, and straight into the kitchen, with its wide bay window, and its warm, welcoming atmosphere. The side door was convenient to bring groceries straight into the kitchen.

Mom and Dad imagined themselves closer to the city, but when they saw the house, its view of the water, its old pool built in the thirties, very art deco, they imagined their daughters running everywhere, happy and free. Dad remembered coming to the beaches of Saint-Eustache when he was a little boy. They saw themselves receiving their friends on the terrace for barbecues. Dad fell in love. He wanted it. Again, as life is full of happy coincidences, he learned that his mother was a friend of Mrs. Paradis. He would manage to acquire it for a good price.

The cottage was the first to be built on the street. All around, there were only cottages that were transformed one by one into houses to be inhabited year-round. We left the city at a time when people were more and more attracted to suburban life. We would be no exception. This is where our story would begin. Dad chose well, it would be our family home for the next forty years!

THE KITCHEN

The kitchen was truly the heart of the house. Its yellow colour and the bay window overlooking the front of the house gave it a warm feeling. For my mother, the bay window was a double-edged sword: she could see who was at the door, but if they happened to be an unwanted guest, she had nowhere to hide.

This was not an open-concept kitchen, which wasn't very common in those days. The idea was that the kitchen had to be hidden because cooking could get really messy. The room was big enough to have a table for five where we ate most of our meals. The dining room was reserved for special occasions, but it wasn't as cozy. As a housewife, my mom thought of the kitchen a little bit like her office space, where she reigned supreme. Things always had to be done her way, so it was always hard to help her when she was cooking. But her cooking was always a highlight of our days. The smells emanating from that kitchen always filled our hearts.

The first renovation came some time in the seventies. The cabinets were covered in a darker, caramel wood, and the walls were a flowery tapestry, which was fashionable at the time. When this went out of style, the tapestry was changed to a yellowy off-white colour. With each passing decade, the kitchen would get a fresh new look, but it always retained its cozy atmosphere and its role as the heart of the house.

Mom spent most of her time in the kitchen, even when she wasn't cooking. Her friends—Mady, Denise, Jocelyne, Suzanne, and Florence—were never far away. They would be found on the small bench at the other end of the room, where the phone was. They each took turns at the other end of the line. They constantly had to tell each other about their husbands, their children, life, and current topics.

THE LIVING ROOM AND ITS PIANO

During the first of many renovations in the seventies, we discovered an electric board linked to each room of the house. We imagined that in the past, a valet tended to an elderly lady's needs in every corner of the house. The panel no longer worked, but there were still two bells there. This setup was ripe for some practical jokes. One of Dad's pleasures was to make me his accomplice when playing tricks. He rang the bell, hidden behind a curtain in his room. It rang downstairs at the front door. He asked Mom to answer. Mom often had her hands in the dough, in the middle of preparing a meal, and wondered why Dad didn't respond. She rushed to the door, opened it, and exclaimed, "There is no one here!" She ran to the back door at the other end of the house and when she realized that there was no one there either, she began to understand and exclaimed, "Urgh! Jeaaan!!!" And Dad and I laughed like maniacs while Mom went back to her kitchen a little irritated. Standing in the living room, this was the first memory that came to my mind.

During this first renovation, the large living room was annexed to the family living room. It had large windows from which you could get lost in the water of the lake. We sat there more often when we had guests.

Our grand piano adorned this large living room. Mom dreamed of hearing us play. I took lessons for five years. I did okay, but I have to admit that I had a softer spot for Elton John's songs than I did for Chopin. Unfortunately, my teacher specialized in classical music, which I hardly enjoyed at ten years old! I preferred playing outside with my friends rather than practising. But Carole, my eldest sister, much prefered piano practice. She would even become a teacher for a while!

She could be heard playing the piano at all hours of the day, sometimes even at seven in the morning! The awakening could be brutal when she got mad at herself for missing a note of Chopin or Beethoven and decided to punch it. After that, it was difficult to go back to sleep. But most of the time when she played, it was comforting, soothing, and it made you dream!

Today, forty years later, in my house, I often play Alexandra Stréliski, telling myself that my mother would also have loved to play her in a loop in her kitchen and living room. Soon, I'm going to get a small grand piano, and I will start performing Chopin again. And I won't be in a hurry to go play outside. Time does wonders!

DAD'S ARRIVAL

Supper time was approaching. The smells of Mom's delicious meals were emanating from the kitchen, and we all wondered what was in store for that night's meal.

Dad arrived around six o'clock through the front door. He closed the door behind him and took a few steps to enter the living room. He swapped his jacket and tie for his beige cardigan sweater. Office style made way for casual style. Dad was always well dressed. I don't mean that he followed the latest fashion styles, but he was always clean looking. He never wore jeans. His office wear included a starch white shirt, a tie, cufflinks, and a pocket handkerchief. On the weekends, he put on his nice wool sweaters, either green or yellow with a scarf around his neck. The final touch, for special occasions at home, was his Knize Ten cologne, a large bottle that his brother sent him from Paris.

Dad looked up to face the two large bay windows with a view of the lake. He felt that he could finally rest from his day. We came to say hello to him. He headed to his sacred La-Z-Boy in the family living room. Mom told him about the adventures of the day. She cut a green apple in four for him and he had a short nap while she prepared dinner. We received orders from Mom not to disturb him. He had removed his office suit and now he had to make the mental transition to family mode!

Back then, the contrast between a man's appearance during a business day and in the evening with his family was quite striking. Today, I rarely see men wear ties, and since Covid hit, I rarely see people getting dressed up for work like my father used to. As for the La-Z-Boy, I don't have one today, but I am thinking about it. My sister and I often fought to sit on it because our feet would be up and the back of the chair could give you a massage.

FAMILY ROOM

Once the dinner was finished we spent a good part of the evening in front of the TV, the central activity of this living room, as is the custom in most North American households. Dad had the remote control. Sometimes, when we were lucky, we managed to influence him on what to watch.

A lot of memories are packed into this little space.

We would cheer on our national hockey team, the Montreal Canadiens, and we would jump for joy when the host exclaimed, "He shoots and scooooores!" Back then, all of Canada was glued to their TV when *Hockey Night in Canada* was on. Football and baseball were also popular, but nothing got us excited like hockey.

The Montreal Canadiens is the hockey team that has won the most Stanley Cups (twenty-four times!), and when I was a kid they won almost every year. When they won it was also a victory for us. They made us feel like winners. Somehow we felt like our positive energy had been instrumental in their win. We felt we had played a part in it. This is one of the subtle ways I felt an egregore at work, even though I wouldn't have thought of it that way at the time.

On Sundays, Mom watched *Les Beaux Dimanches* ("Beautiful Sundays"), hoping to raise our intellectual and cultural education a little. We loved watching *Quelle famille* ("What a family"). We found things that brought us together when we dreamed of being a larger family like them. Coming back from school, I rushed with my snack to watch *Bobino*, and if I was lucky, I got to watch *Belle et Sébastien* with my sister, and we imagined ourselves in the arms of Sébastien. Thirty years later, I got a dog that looks like Belle; she is now twelve years old. And I made my life with Martin instead of Sébastien!

THE STORM

1971. It was a stormy November evening. Nature was raging outside. The branches of trees banged against the window as if to say, "Let me in!" The lake looked like it was about to swallow us whole. The thunder rumbled, and the lightning burst as though God was angry. All the lights in the house went out at the same time. No electricity. I felt like I was in a haunted house.

I was scared to death. I went down the steps to find myself in the living room with my parents. I was quickly followed by my two big sisters, who looked scared too. My parents kept a cool head and decided on a plan of action. Mom took out the flashlights and candles. With the electricity out, the temperature in the house went way down. To preserve the heat, Mom closed the curtains that separated the two living rooms, and Dad prepared a fire in the fireplace. I helped him by balling up newspapers as he taught me. I was proud to be helpful.

We helped Mom turn the sofa into a bed. We went to get sheets and the large beige wool blanket from Hudson's Bay. It was prickly, but it was by far the warmest one we had. We had nothing to distract ourselves but the sound of our voices, which was calming in a way. Mom told me to try to sleep. Usually, I never liked bedtime, because I had to miss the end of an episode, or a movie, and I found myself alone on the top floor. But that time, it was different. I felt safe between my two big sisters, and I fell asleep looking at Dad's fire; he made the most beautiful fires!

This special moment abruptly came to an end when the lights came back on, blinding us, and the purring of the fridge resumed. Dad carried me to my bed. The storm was over, and so was our living room camping adventure. The next morning, the routine would resume.

Today, I love storms. Unfortunately, we rarely run out of electricity. So rare are our evenings of camping in the living room. Still, each lit fireplace or storm transports me to this living room with my family. Somewhere, I'm still five years old, and a cozy feeling overwhelms me!

NAMASTE

One evening when I got home, I walked through the living room and found myself in front of Dad lying on the ground, looking lifeless. I panicked and shouted, "Mooooom!" She ran out of the kitchen and my father was resurrected immediately! All three of us almost had a heart attack—me who thought Dad was dead, Mom who heard my screams, and Dad rather angry to come back to life.

Poor Dad. He had had heart problems and was exploring ways to reduce his stress. He read a lot about yoga. The practice was considered rather "hippie" (or "granola" as we said back then), so he practised it discreetly, in private. It was far from the style of his generation, but Dad was curious and always looking for solutions. That day, as the house was empty, he had decided to practice the pose of the Savasana, also known as the corpse pose. He did it so well that I got caught up in the game, and I'm sure on that day it did not meet the desired effect of relaxing him.

Today, to calm my nerves, I follow in his tracks. Sometimes it's through meditation classes in motion like tai chi and other times it's also Savasana, but I always make sure there will be no interruption or unexpected visitors!

THE VEGETABLE GARDEN

Summer 1970. I was five years old. When I came home from school, Mom asked for my help to work in the garden, in the large field in front of the house. Pulling out the weeds was tedious and not my favourite activity, but when Mom asked, I obeyed. I kneeled in the vegetable garden to pull out the weeds with her, then planted seeds, and a few days later, I discovered strawberries, cucumbers, and vegetables of all kinds that I had fun picking, sometimes for dinner and sometimes just for me! I would often cut a chives stalk and pretend that I had a cigarette in my mouth like an adult, except that I eventually ate it.

In the winter, our vegetable garden turned into an ice rink. My sister Jo had an innate talent at ice-skating. When she did it, she was on top of the world! She did pirouettes and acrobatics to dazzle us. My sister Carole and I were entertained and in admiration. We didn't have her talent.

My sisters grew up, my mother got older, the big vegetable garden got smaller and then disappeared. It was replaced by sprawling grass and became the blueprint of the vegetable gardens my sisters and I would later have in our own homes.

THE NEIGHBOURHOOD

The neighbourhood was made up of all different kinds of houses—small and large, old cottages and new houses... What made the neighbourhood's identity was not really the architecture of its houses. It was the *joie de vivre* of the children who inhabited them!

Nowadays, I am also friends with my neighbours. We don't play rope together, but we eat, laugh, and dance together. Of course, we live in a different society today, and people sometimes apologize for coming over unannounced. But I love it, because I feel like I'm ten years old again, and friends are asking me to come and play with them. Back then, we didn't have cell phones, so we would just show up at our friends' houses to see if they wanted to do something. I guess now it's expected that someone will text before coming over. But I do enjoy the unexpected surprise of a neighbour coming by just to hang out and keep current.

When I was a kid, no one locked their doors. There was no anxiety about children getting kidnapped. Kids weren't asked to wear a helmet when they rode their bikes. It was a time of great freedom for children.

One of my neighbour friends, when I was a kid, was Richard. One day, I went to his house because he had just gotten a new set of drums. He was really good at it, and everyone took turns playing. I didn't know Richard that well, and I felt shy. But I did look through his record collection, because I felt like it was a great way to get to know someone and break the ice. I found many records I knew and loved, but then I came across a yellow record I had never seen before. Genesis… I knew their song "Follow You, Follow Me," but nothing more. Richard was surprised that I didn't know them, so he asked everyone to stop playing the drums, and he put on the record, entitled *A Trick of the Tail*. And that was when I fell in love with Genesis. I bought the album the next day. It played in my room over and over again. Every time I had a party, "Ripples" was always on the playlist. Many years later, I have lost touch with Richard. But I still think of him every time I listen to Genesis, and I am grateful for him introducing me to them.

LEAVING HOME

I really had an idyllic childhood, but I was still too young to realize it. I dreamed of fleeing the countryside and experiencing the buzz of the city. I tried to convince my father to abandon the countryside and move to the city, but he told me that people lived longer in rural areas. Living old? I was seventeen years old! I had my whole life ahead of me. I didn't realize the importance of his words. Again, he was right. He survived all his family and friends, by several years. Was it the calm of the place that surrounded him or the result of chance? I'm inclined to believe it was a nice mix of both!

When I left home, I finally lived in the heart of downtown Montreal on Sherbrooke Street in an apartment that made me feel like I was in New York. I loved it, but to be honest, I was so used to a spacious home that I sometimes felt stifled. My father would call me just in time.

The phone rang. My father was now retired, and he who never even knew how to cook an egg started taking cooking classes. My theory was that he used cooking as bait to attract us back home. And it worked! I was fine in my city buzz, but when I found myself back in my childhood home, it was like an escape to another world. When my father invited me, I would often hit the road a few minutes after getting off the phone.

MY WEDDING

August 2002. I was getting married in the house I grew up in. For sentimental reasons and for the pretty scenery, I never wanted to get married anywhere else. It was a beautiful way to immortalize my childhood home in my memory, just like my eldest sister did almost twenty years earlier for her own wedding.

There was another reason I wanted to get married here. I

had a hunch that my parents would not keep the house for too much longer. Getting married here felt like a nice way to tie up loose ends. Dad talked more and more about the offers he had on the house. He was flattered but didn't think he would sell it just yet. But I still had the impression that he was seriously considering the idea.

My wedding theme song was a little-known song by Aznavour, "Ma main a besoin de ta main," ("My hand needs your hand") because of the lyrics and because it was in this house that Aznavour's music rocked my childhood.

It was a great summer day. Rain was forecast, but, as though by magic, the showers only began when the last guest, my friend Paul, left us at two o'clock in the morning. I couldn't have asked for a more beautiful day, having all the people I cherished in the place I loved the most. It was the greatest gift that providence could give me!

THE DEPARTURE

January 2003. Mom and Dad were getting older. Dad wanted to spend the rest of his days at the house, but Mom wanted to go and live in a condo. She was tired of living in a house full of memories, with too many empty rooms and not enough life. She wanted to move on to a new chapter of her life. My sisters and I didn't understand her.

"Why would you ever want to move?" I asked her one day.

"I feel like I'm staying in a house with ghosts," she answered. "I walk past your room and your sister's rooms, and you're not there anymore. You are living your own lives now. I want to live mine."

I could feel the emotion in her voice. All of a sudden, I understood her point of view.

My sisters and I no longer lived here, but we wanted our parents to keep the house. How selfish of us, when you really think about it. Maybe it was a way for us to hold on to our childhood memories. Mom was tired, and we refused to see it. Dad was starting to get frail. Mom was scared but didn't talk about it.

After this exchange, I understood. I understood that it was time for me to let go of the past and trust the present and the future, and especially it was time for me to help Mom and Dad in this new chapter, in this transition.

We visited condos and found out that there were other beautiful places to live. They found a place, moved there, and life went on.

TURNING A CORNER

May 10, 2003, 3:01 p.m. The moving truck turned the corner, and I followed it a few minutes later.

In a few seconds I relived the springs, autumns, winters, and summers that I lived through in this house, as well as the births, the joys, the sorrows, the small and large celebrations.

A childhood home for me is like a first love. We can never repeat it, but we must leave room for other loves, new dreams, new adventures.

I tried to imagine myself keeping it and living there, but I quickly realized that its charm depended on the presence and warmth of my parents. Without them, it is only a house just like any other house: four walls and some grass.

Their presence made it a home, a place where you wanted to be.

Every house has its own history. This one was unique. It drew its soul, its essence, from Jean and Gisèle. They are the reason that I will have the house's street number—number 32—forever tattooed on my heart.

TWENTY YEARS LATER

Today, the house is demolished, the pool is buried, the address is no longer there. The house is gone and so have my parents, but not the magic of life and my story.

My husband is the barbecue pro, and I try to recreate my mother's recipes. For special occasions, I concoct my father's marshmallow dessert, which we loved, called marshmallow bites[3]. It was his bait to make us come to him! My theory is that my father dreamed of being an Italian mama who manages, through her good food, to keep her family always united and very close at heart. (The funny thing is that when I took a DNA test, it showed I was seven point four percent Italian. I am very proud of that. It's not much, but I'll take it!)

Dad succeeded in his endeavour, because today, family reunions are perpetuated, always around a good meal at the same table that used to be in the dining room at my childhood home. The same table where, as a child, I tried to stretch my little leg to ring the bell in order to make the whole family laugh. The difference is that today, my legs are longer, the bells are no longer there, and I am the one who sits at the end, instead of Mom, along with my husband, instead of Dad.

I had my first house, my first cottage, a holiday by the sea… My set of criteria is based on this first love. Wherever I go, I must have water, old tall trees, friendly neighbours, lots of green space, and a window beside my bed through which I can look before falling asleep and when I wake up.

The old house is a symbol. The pain fades. Life, love, friends, family, everything changes, transforms… We create new memories and we continue our story!

---

3. See Recipes: Marshmallow bites (p. 223)

PENNY FOR YOUR THOUGHTS

Have you ever had to say goodbye to your childhood home?
How did that make you feel? Close your eyes and make a
mental map of that house. Picture yourself walking through
every room. What was your happiest memory in each room
of the house? What was your favourite room? What smells
do you remember coming from the kitchen? What games did
you play? Did you carry any traditions over to the present
day? What does your current home have in common with
your childhood home?

CHAPTER 7

A LADLEFUL OF LOVE

Cooking is love made visible.

—ANONYMOUS

PLAYLIST

Des croissants de soleil · GINETTE RENO
Le petit pain au chocolat · JOE DASSIN
Mambo Italiano · DEAN MARTIN
All That Meat and Potatoes · LOUIS ARMSTRONG
Coconut Christmas · THE LOST FINGERS
Café corsé · BLEU JEANS BLEU
Love Is · ADAM COHEN
Sur ma vie · CHARLES AZNAVOUR
Jardin d'hiver · HENRI SALVADOR
Le frigidaire · TEX LECOR
La bohème · CHARLES AZNAVOUR
T'es belle · JEAN-PIERRE FERLAND
Le p'tit bonheur · FÉLIX LECLERC
La vie en rose · ÉDITH PIAF

I sometimes wonder what funny things people inherit from their parents. It was a cold October day, and my husband, my son, and I could all feel that winter was coming. I was wondering what to cook for dinner and the words "soup" and "comfort food" kept resonating in my mind.

I used the last herbs I got from my garden along with its last carrots and cherry tomatoes. Just like my mom would cook an empty-fridge soup, I decided to cook an empty-garden soup.[4] I started with my herbs—rosemary, lemon thyme, chive, sage, a little mint—and I added them all in my organic chicken broth, mixed with a little bit of spinach and endives. With a little bit of herbal salt, pepper, and lemon, it tasted great. Time to serve!

I took out my favourite soup ladle. One of the few objects I still have from my Mom. It's funny the things we keep from the people we love. It's probably worth five cents on the market, but to me, it's priceless. It is my greatest reminder of how my mom took good care of us through her cooking. Her go-to when we were sick, when she needed to empty the fridge, or on cold October days, was always to make some soup to give us a little bit of comfort.

The meals she prepared were not out of the ordinary at that time in Quebec, but she always put interesting spins on the food. Her roast beef was covered in Dijon mustard with

4. See Recipes: Empty fridge vegetable soup (p. 225)

a side of Béarnaise sauce, green peas cooked in a rich cream with onions, sliced carrots in garlic butter, and her mashed potatoes with milk, cream, butter, and onions.

When Mom was cooking, she would often start with a recipe book but would not follow the recipe all the way through. She had great instinct. She would see something missing from the recipe and add it in—garlic, new spices…

In those days, religion was omnipresent, and a lot of recipe books were written by nuns. They gave a lot of cooking lessons, and wrote a lot of cookbooks. They also hosted a lot of cooking shows on TV.

My mom was health conscious before it was cool. In the mornings, she would sometimes cook me oatmeal, which I hated. Once, my dad looked in my bowl and said, "Ewww! Oatmeal! Gross! It tastes awful! I remember eating it when I was in the army. It tastes like glue! Never again! Anyway, have a nice day." And off he went, leaving my mother to look crestfallen. She suggested I add brown sugar on top to make it more palatable.

Mom's cooking was often inspired by French cuisine, with a lot of rich foods made with cream and butter. The French tend to eat big meals for lunch, but lighter meals for dinner, because they know that the afternoon activities will help them burn all the lunch-time calories. And that's how the French are able to eat hearty meals without gaining a lot of weight. But that's not really how things are in Quebec. We took the culinary influence from France, but we were originally farmers, so the big meals were not for lunch but for dinner. Being in a country with so much distance, we did not walk everywhere like the Europeans did, we had to take the car. Despite the French inspiration, my mother would always put a typically Canadian spin on her meals.

Food was how my mother showed her love and her passion. Unfortunately, as the decades passed, society was putting less and less importance on the roles of mothers in the home, and as a result my mother seemed to find shame in the fact that she was a housewife. It's so unfortunate because I truly recall her as the most important person in the house. If it wasn't for her, my dad probably wouldn't have been as successful a businessman as he ended up being. Having a stable home life, he was free to focus on his work and on being a great dad.

When we had big parties with thirty guests for the holidays, Mom would lay out the fruits of her labour in a buffet—beautifully presented meals that everyone always complimented her on. On Easter, we would have ham with maple syrup and pineapples. At Thanksgiving and Christmas, it was turkey with gravy with Mom's amazing mashed potato stuffing!

My mother's cooking got me through tough times. Whenever I had a bad day and came home to a great meal, I was already half-way cured from my case of the blues. Mom made the best roast beefs, mashed potatoes, lots of spaghetti, and so many wonderful dishes. It was the wonderful smell of her food that made us happy to come to her when she called our names from down the stairs. When we came home from school, the kitchen was always our first stop. We would grab food on our way to the living room to watch TV. We could find anything our heart desired in that kitchen. The freezer was packed with spaghetti meat sauce; cretons meat paté; meat and vegetarian lasagna; strawberry, rhubarb, and blueberry jams; apple sauce... In the cupboard, you could find her homemade ketchup and pickled cucumbers, among many other things.

Mom spent most of her day in the kitchen, even when she wasn't actually cooking. She would read, talk on the phone, and play bridge there. You might say that my mother's favourite space was the kitchen, even if she wouldn't want to admit it. She had a love-hate relationship with the room. It was her friend and her enemy at the same time. She was a fantastic cook but she was passionate about so many other things. Like many women of her generation, she would have liked not to be confined to a single activity.

I also remember that wasting food was a big no-no in those days. Mom was from a family of modest means, so if there was leftover roast beef, we would have roast beef sandwiches the next day. If we had veggies for one dinner, the leftovers would turn into soup the following day. Nothing ever went to waste. My parents were from a time where you just don't throw things away. Clothes that had holes in them would be mended.

So when I picked up that soup ladle, preparing a nice soup to warm up my family's hearts, I was reminded that even though Mom had been gone for over twelve years by then, I still honoured her memory (sometimes unconsciously) by cooking dinner every night and comforting my family with a hot soup. It was a way for me to show my love, as my mother had shown me hers.

PENNY FOR YOUR THOUGHTS

What importance does food have in your family? Your friends? What do you consider your best comfort food? What food reminds you of your parents? Do you have an object that means a lot to you that belonged to your parents?

CHAPTER 8

MY MARY POPPINS

*Mary Poppins herself had flown away, but the gifts
she had brought would remain for always.*

—P. L. TRAVERS

PLAYLIST

Supercalifragilisticexpialidocious · JULIE ANDREWS
A Spoonful of Sugar · JULIE ANDREWS
I Love to Laugh · JULIE ANDREWS
Jolly Holiday · DICK VAN DYKE AND JULIE ANDREWS
Stay Awake · JULIE ANDREWS

The other day I went to my favourite dry cleaner. He's a good guy, really friendly. He remembers my name, chats with me, and everything I bring him comes back looking practically new. Even better, he is the only one in my area who is eco-friendly. We often start chatting when I pick up my clothes. In these pandemic times, it feels good to socialize. While discussing nothing and everything, he finally tells me his last name and where he lives, and we realize that he is the little nephew of my favourite babysitter from a very, very long time ago. It really is a small world!

On the way back, I started thinking about that old babysitter. Memories of her were tucked away in a forgotten drawer inside my head. I often think back to when my son was little or even my adolescence, but when I think of my child-hood, it seems so far away that it really feels like another life, almost like a dream.

I started smiling…

In the seventies, Dad worked like crazy. Mom managed the house, the three children, the two cats, the two dogs, and my father's stress when he came home. (At this point, he had already had a heart attack, and she wanted to keep him healthy for a long time.) Her job was to keep balance and happiness at home, to make the house a home. She had her hands full, and she would have liked to have some time for herself, to breathe.

She hired a housekeeper, Madame Nadon. Around sixty

years old, Madame Nadon was a short woman with short black hair, brown eyes, red lipstick and nails. She could be strict, but she had a heart of gold and a strong sense of responsibility. She would do much more than cleaning, becoming a kind of "trusted woman." The whole family loved her. She was a really good person, honest and endearing. In a way, she became my adoptive grandmother.

I remember one April Fools' Day, she helped me put on my coat, telling me that I had to hurry so as not to miss the bus. Once I got to school, I found a paper fish sticking behind my back. I thought it was very funny. I couldn't wait to come home to get my revenge. She pretended she didn't see me doing it, and she laughed with me. She was young at heart. I loved it.

When my parents went out she was the one who looked after me. She cooked me good dinners, but it was her dessert that I remember the most: her Chomeur's pudding.[5] What a delight! I loved it when Madame Nadon looked after me because she showed me a lot of games. We played a lot of Chinese checkers, regular checkers, and card games. One of my favourite card games was War. One day she brought home a big square wooden board for us. Her son had made holes in it, and she had painted a heart, a clover, a diamond, and a spade on it. Sometimes we would just play one-on-one. Other times my sisters would join us. We laughed so much.

She came every week to help with the housework. Sometimes, when I arrived from school, I met her husband, who was waiting for her in his car. He was a taxi driver and

---

5. See Recipes: Chomeur's pudding (p. 226)

had finished his shift. I was excited when I saw him because he was really nice. He would chat with me and always offered me a piece of Chiclet gum, which he always had plenty of. They were small packets with two pieces of gum inside. Every time, I prayed that he would still have a red one—the cherry one—it was the best. But, when I was unlucky, only yellow ones were left—the bland ones. It usually meant that my sister had gotten to it before me!

One day my parents left us in the care of Madame Nadon. My sisters went to see their friends and came home for dinner. When we were young, we liked to play tricks on each other. In the evening, we each went to our rooms to put on our pajamas and dressing gowns so that we could watch TV for longer. That night, I was faster than my older sister Carole. I quickly ran to the top of the stairs, put on my pajamas, and hid in her wardrobe, between her very fashionable earth-coloured clothes, with flowers and peace signs (my sister was a bit of a hippie). It was hard because I was afraid of the dark, and also because I really wanted to laugh. I managed to hold back for a few seconds. Carole opened her wardrobe door, and I shouted, "Boo!" She screamed, and I rolled to the floor laughing. I did it! Me, The Flea (that's what they called me because I was the smallest one), the one who was eight years younger, I managed to surprise my big sister! I was really proud of myself. My sister, not so much. I didn't understand. I thought she would find it funny. My other sister Jo, on the other hand, did find it very funny. Carole was furious. She looked like she wanted to tear my head off. Fortunately, Madame Nadon was coming. I was saved. Poor Madame Nadon almost had a heart attack when she heard my sister scream.

A few days passed. On another quiet evening, Madame Nadon was in the sewing room, where Mom's sewing machine was (this was also where we did our homework).

She called me, telling me to put on my pajamas. I went up the steps, brushed my teeth in the red bathroom, and headed to my small yellow room. I put on my pajamas and took three steps towards my tiny wardrobe. It was barely as high as I was, and I was pretty small myself. Now keep in mind that I was afraid of monsters, often wondering if they existed. Obviously, I thought about them especially in the evening, when it was dark. I told myself that if they were lurking somewhere, it would be either in my wardrobe or under my bed. I nervously opened my wardrobe. I barely touched the handle as the door opened, and a monster showed up in front of me. I screamed bloody murder! My heart was beating at full speed! I ran away until I was out of breath. The monster started laughing out loud. It was tall and had long blond hair. It was Carole! She was very proud of herself. She got her revenge. Madame Nadon almost had her second heart attack in a few days. She entered my room, and I jumped into her arms. She comforted me. Somehow, it was funnier when I was the one doing the tricks!

BATMAN

It was a sunny and warm summer day, and my parents had left for the week, leaving us in the care of Madame Nadon. Night fell, and we were all going to bed. All of a sudden, I heard noises, I heard screams. I woke up startled. Madame Nadon picked me up from my room and ordered me to go outside with my two sisters. We stood at a really far distance from the house. I didn't really understand what was going on. I was half asleep. I saw Madame Nadon coming in and out of the house with a broom. Was she playing the witch or something? My sister explained to me that a bat had entered the house and Madame Nadon was trying to get it out, but she was having a hard time. I was afraid, and feeling the energy of my sisters, I knew that I was not the only one. Fortunately, I could hide between the two.

I admired Madame Nadon so much; she was not afraid of anything. But she was still struggling to get the bat out of the house. She called her son Yvan, who would come to save us from the bat. We three girls were quite pleased because we loved Yvan very much. He was handsome, nice, and he took us on boat rides! So he came over and got rid of the bat in no time. To comfort us, he promised that he would take us on his boat the next day! Thank God for bats! We went back to bed to have sweet dreams about the next day with Yvan!

The week came to an end, and my parents came back, glad we were left in good hands. Madame Nadon spent the next week getting a good rest. Looking after us was probably not very relaxing for her.

I have fond memories of my adoptive grandmother. As the years passed, I needed a babysitter less and less. I grew up. We went on with our lives. She came to say hello a few times. She saw that I was getting older, but I didn't see that she was getting older. Her husband got sick and she took care of him. We heard less and less from her, and one day, nothing.

Madame Nadon wasn't in our lives for very long, but she was there for the pivotal years. When you're a child, you don't particularly like being away from your parents. But with her, I felt safe, I felt loved and protected. I spent some wonderful days with her, and I think she did too. She didn't fly or sing, so she wasn't quite Mary Poppins—but almost!

Family and friends are important. But in a day, in a lifetime, there are also other people who make a difference. The caretaker, the baker, the dry cleaner…

During Covid, we couldn't see our families or our friends, but we could still meet people who make a difference in our lives.

By the way, I do not know where you are today Madame Nadon, I just wanted to say: Thank you.

PENNY FOR YOUR THOUGHTS

Did you have someone besides your parents who helped take care of you as a kid? Maybe a babysitter, a relative, or a friend of your parents', who had a role to play in who you are today? If you could thank someone for making your childhood better, who would it be? Did you ever hide and scare a brother or a sister? If you could thank a local store owner who makes you smile, who would it be?

CHAPTER 9

THE VALENTINE'S DAY TRADITION

*Tradition is the means by which the vitality of the
past enriches the life of the present.*

—T. S. ELIOT

PLAYLIST

Le plus fort c'est mon père · LYNDA LEMAY
Because You Loved Me · CÉLINE DION
Parler à mon père · CÉLINE DION
Ma fille · ISABELLE BOULAY
Oh toi mon père · NICOLA CICCONE
Daughters · JOHN MAYER
Brown Eyed Girl · VAN MORRISON
My Father's Eyes · ERIC CLAPTON
Father's Eyes · AMY GRANT
Mon père à moi · GILBERT BÉCAUD
Mon père disait · JACQUES BREL
Les yeux de mon père · MICHEL SARDOU
Sur les épaules de mon père · ANGELINA
Dis papa · GEORGES GUÉTARY
À ma fille · CHARLES AZNAVOUR

Valentine's Day. I was six or maybe seven years old. I woke up to the sun illuminating my yellow room. I was super excited because I loved Valentine's Day. The day before, I wrote my little Valentine's cards to distribute to all my favourite friends. Card is a big word. They were little bright red hearts made of paper with cartoon animals on them (a bunny or an elephant), adorned with little phrases like, "Will you be my Valentine?" I was excited, but also a little nervous; I hoped my friends would say yes to being my Valentines! Especially Benoît!

I got dressed quickly and went down the stairs. Before breakfast every morning, I sat on the yellow chair, and Mom made my ponytails. During the day, I had fun swinging them from left to right. I ate corn flakes quickly and I drank the freshly squeezed orange juice Mom just made me. I hurried up. I couldn't wait to go to school!

I ran to the front door to put on my ugly but warm and practical boots. I put on my yellow Ski-doo coat, not great looking but it kept me warm. Anyway I had no choice, my mother was the one who dressed me! To finish things off, she wrapped me up in a red scarf that she knitted for me, which went from Montreal to New York! So I wasn't afraid to get cold while I climbed the snowbanks to play the queen of the mountain in my warm clothes!

I was in my first year at the small school in the neighbourhood. I had lots of friends, and I loved school. My teachers were really nice and my classmates were too. I was often first in class because I loved my teacher. Class was always fun at that time. I took the bus every morning in front of the church. Mr. Roy, the driver, was the one who brought me back home at lunchtime. He was also the owner of the Chalet, the neighbourhood snack bar and our favourite hangout. When Mom was not at home at lunchtime, I jumped for joy because I knew I was going to eat the best burger with fries, and as a dessert I'd have a brown bag full of one-cent candy! Pushing the orange doors of the Chalet to go sit on a small red seat from which I could admire the wall of candy in front of me, gorging myself with sweets, this was my definition of happiness! On the rare occasions when I had a quarter to play the pinball machine, I was in heaven.

The day before Valentine's Day, I went there and bought candy hearts. They came in pastel yellow, white, pink, and blue, with a message written on them, like "Be mine," "XOXO," or "Smile." You could only get them on Valentine's Day. I couldn't wait to give them to my friends!

I arrived at school. On entering my class, there was a row of pints on the edge of the wall. I had to make my choice: orange juice, chocolate milk, or lemonade. I quickly chose chocolate milk. I ran to sit at my desk. The teacher pulled out the TV for us to watch kid shows. The actors spoke to us directly. They could see us and would ask us questions that we all answered in unison. Then Mrs. Garneau, my teacher whom I loved, gave us a little test, and then came recess. I gave my Valentine's cards, and I got a lot of them in return. It's nice to know that we are loved!

Almost everyone in the class knew that I had a crush on Benoît, and I learned that it was mutual! We made little smiles at each other, and sometimes we exchanged a few words and looks—another small source of happiness.

At lunchtime, little bullies decided that Benoît and I were going to kiss. We were both kidnapped, and suddenly, we found ourselves face to face with people who were heckling and pushing. I refused and ran away. I didn't like being forced to do anything, even at seven years old. Benoît felt the same way, but I think he was still hoping we would kiss. I was probably sending him the wrong message by running away, but all that aggressive pushing was not very romantic… I liked to dream of Benoît, exchange smiles, words, looks, but from there to kissing? Eeek! That's for adults. Sometimes the dream is more attractive than the act!

We went back to class. I was a little sad. I wondered if Benoît would still love me. We were no longer exchanging smiles or looks. Love is hard. The class ended, and I went home. On the bus I talked with my friend Lizanne and discussed plans to see each other the following weekend.

I arrived home and played a little outside, making a snowman. When I eventually got cold, I went back inside, hoping I hadn't missed my TV program. The man on TV also spoke directly to me as he could see through the screen! Then it was homework time and I worked on the kitchen table while Mom prepared dinner.

It was 6 p.m. I heard the front door. It was Dad. I ran to join him and give him a kiss. I was glad to see him. He had gifts! One for every woman in the family (which is all of us).

Four red velvet hearts from Laura Secord, full of chocolates. Mom was lucky because she got the biggest one.

Dad walked to the blue sofa, swapped his office jacket for his beige cardigan, and took off his tie. He was now in his comfy home-sweet-home attire. He went to give Mom a kiss in the kitchen and asked her if we were having dinner soon. She told him he would have time to take a little nap on his chair. His La-Z-Boy. The Boss's chair. The one that was a source of tug-of-war a few minutes earlier between my sister and me to watch TV, because by pushing a small button, you can find yourself comfortable with your feet in the air. My sister and I had to slip away to leave Dad in peace. Then Mom brought him a green apple, cut into quarters, so that he would not starve. After his nap, he listened to the news. Mom prepared a roast beef with mashed potatoes, carrots with garlic butter, and Béarnaise sauce. When it was ready, she called us for supper. Carole, my older sister, who was reading, came out of her room. The five of us sat around the table and told each other about our days.

After dessert, we got up from the table and headed to the sofa in front of the TV. We watched *The Sound of Music*, with Friedrich, whom I also had a crush on. This helped me forget Benoît momentarily!

I sat on Dad's lap. I was so happy with my chocolates. This was our tradition every Valentine's Day. Dad never forgot. I fell asleep on him. I loved him. He was the only man in my life!

Dad is no longer with us. But I still buy those chocolates in his memory. The Laura Secord stores have been around since 1913, so there is every reason to believe that my grandfather may have been doing the same for his children and his wife. Thirty years later, I continue the tradition. Every year I buy a Laura Secord heart for my son and for my husband. It's a big box of dark chocolates from Daniel Gendron. The best in the world! Artisanal and made in Quebec, it's happiness in a box!

Tastes are changing, but the important thing is tradition. Every time I go into a Laura Secord store, I feel like I'm with my dad. Every Valentine's Day, when I give my chocolates, I feel that he is still with me. He still lives because he lives through me, through traditions. Maybe one day it will be my son's turn to become his daughter's idol, for a lifetime.

PENNY FOR YOUR THOUGHTS

Are there any traditions that are dear to you and your family? Do you ever think of starting them again now? It doesn't have to be something big or grandiose! What is your favourite treat? What is your favourite chocolate?

CHAPTER 10

THE CAMP: A PARENT'S DUTY

Joy in looking and comprehending is nature's most beautiful gift.

—ALBERT EINSTEIN

PLAYLIST

You've Got a Friend · JAMES TAYLOR
Suspicious Minds · ELVIS PRESLEY
Father and Son · YUSUF CAT STEVENS
Gone Gone Gone · PHILLIP PHILLIPS
Leaving on a Jet Plane · JOHN DENVER
Mrs. Robinson · SIMON AND GARFUNKEL
Tapestry · CAROLE KING
Jolene · DOLLY PARTON
Gypsy · FLEETWOOD MAC
Make it With You · BREAD
Your Song · ELTON JOHN
Blowin' in the Wind · BOB DYLAN
Ventura Highway · AMERICA
Listen to the Music · THE DOOBIE BROTHERS

July 21, 1977. It was eight o'clock in the morning on a hot day. I got in the car with Mom and Dad. I was going to a camp in upstate New York.

My father spoke perfect English just like his parents, and he wanted the same for me. I often told him that one day I would like to be a businesswoman, and he would reply, "Then you will have to speak the language of business: English." My father, a successful entrepreneur, sold across Canada, the United States, and around the world, so he could speak perfectly in both French and English. More than that though, he also wanted me to have other experiences. The Canadian dollar was very strong which allowed my father to enroll me in this camp in the United States. It had been around since 1922, and I had older cousins who had been there. My dad wanted me to learn different sports and get out of my comfort zone, out of my hometown. I resisted the idea, overcome with fear, but my parents did not listen to me. This was well before the era of the child-as-king!

When my father had an idea in mind, he did not let go, and that's why he wanted me to go to this camp in the United States. It was going to be a long drive to New York. I really didn't feel like going. I had a lump in my throat ready to explode. I didn't want to look like a baby, so I tried to control myself. My mind was spinning at full speed, as I tried to appeal to my creativity and intelligence to find the right reason that would convince my parents not to send me that far. I didn't like the idea of being alone in another country in the middle of the forest with strangers, far from my family, my friends, my dogs, and my home. I feared that I would miss some great times back home, and that I would be replaced and forgotten. My parents were also much older than the average parent, so I often worried that something would happen to them.

Dad had a new car. The great luxury was that the radio came with an eight-track player. Ford even gave us a complementary eight-track tape with the best songs of the year. I asked Dad to put it on. I was lucky because my mom and dad knew that they wouldn't have to put up with my requests for the next four weeks, so they were more ready to indulge me than usual. Mom turned up the volume. It was Elvis. I looked outside, where everything was very green. The view eventually put me to sleep.

The car stopped. I woke up in a panic. Mom asked me if I was hungry. I rarely answered this question in the negative. I jumped out of the car to walk into a Howard Johnson's restaurant, a large family restaurant with a bright orange roof, hard to miss. They were everywhere. I picked the macaroni and cheese on the children's menu. I was a little disappointed, it wasn't nearly as good as my mother's cooking. But it was fine because I could catch up on dessert. They offered twenty-eight flavours of ice cream! I asked Mom if I could have a sundae. She said yes. I realized that leaving home for a while had its advantages! I was having a great time, until Dad looked at his watch and reminded us that we had to get back on the road if we wanted to get there on time. I slowed down my eating. I hoped I was going to miss opening time, and maybe they wouldn't be able to accept me, and I would have to go home. Unfortunately for me, Dad was never late.

We arrived. The lump in my throat was more present than ever. I said goodbye to Dad. Mom walked with me to my cabin. Everyone looked nice but very busy. There were ten beds, which all looked equally uncomfortable. Mom exclaimed, "It's beautiful! How fun! You're going to make new friends..." I gave her a dubious look.

I walked her back to the car. I didn't know how I was going to survive. A young woman stopped us, "You must be Elizabeth!" Suddenly, I felt important. She had just interrupted the endless pathos of "poor little old me" which had been spinning in my head for a few hours. She had big blue eyes, beautiful red cheeks, and an endearing smile. She introduced herself; her name was Connie, and she was one of my two instructors. She leaned towards me, spoke softly to me, and invited me to join the others in my group. I said a quick goodbye to Mom. I was sad, but curious at the same time to meet the girls from my cabin. There were people from everywhere. Maria was very embarrassed because she could not speak English; she came from Mexico. Rosa, from Venezuela, was a ball of energy. Christina, also from Venezuela, was a beauty. Kathy and Judy were from New York, Vickie from New Hampshire, Kim from Massachusetts, Suzanne "Miss Sports" was from Montreal and then, there was me. The camp began!

7:15 a.m. We woke up to the sound of the bugle. We walked across the camp in our pajamas to go have breakfast in the dining room, a large wooden hut with a high ceiling. I discovered sugar and cinnamon toast and peanut butter and jam sandwiches. I loved them! We sang songs and played games to remember everyone's names. Everyone had a hard time pronouncing my very French last name, among all these American and Spanish names. It often made me smile. We went back to our cabin, made our bed, got dressed, and prepared for our activities.

I started the day with a swimming class, which I did not particularly enjoy. The lake's water was icy, not particularly clear, and small leeches could be found in some places. I often told myself I would be glad to see the rain, because then swimming would be replaced by a cooking class! While the instructor explained the next type of swimming we would do, I often found myself in a mental horror movie where a barracuda took a good bite off my leg. Nevertheless, I came up every time and passed the next tests to get my next swimming badge. Then I hurried up to get changed and go to my archery class. I liked it very much, because to my surprise I often managed to send my arrow to the middle of the bullseye. I didn't know how I did it, but I liked this feeling of being good at it.

Then I had tennis and horseback riding. I was good at those, but the professor was harsh. I couldn't wait for my water-skiing class. It made me feel free, with my hair in the wind. I concentrated very hard to avoid falling. The image of barracudas was very much alive in my mind, which helped motivate me not to fall! I loved my arts and crafts class. We often made bracelets there. One time, we were instructed to create a work of art with a maple leaf, Crayola wax pencils, parchment paper, and an iron! On my first day in arts and crafts, I had to draw a feather. It was blue. So they put me on the blue team for the Camp Olympics.

Later we had dinner and activities around the fire in the large wooden hut. Everyone was sitting on the floor. We played games in groups. My friends traced letters on my back, and I had to guess what they were. The instructors put on some shows (a bit like at Club Med, but with a lower budget), and my favourite part was when Michelle played the piano and we all sang along. The voices, the fire, the wood, the smiles… It was magical. This was when I discovered Cat Stevens's "Father and Sons," and John Denver's "Take Me Home, Country Roads." And I started telling myself that I never wanted to leave this place. Then we walked in the dark with our flashlights to return to our respective cabins. It was time to go to sleep.

In the morning, we were awoken by Christmas carols. At first, I thought I was dreaming, because it was a hot July day. And now we were celebrating Christmas in July! Female instructors sang, holding candles. It was beautiful. We went down the coast, singing again, but this time, Christmas songs. With the heat and summer atmosphere, I found it weird, but quickly, I was charmed.

On the day of the Camp Olympics, whether I was riding a horse or practicing another sport I had a whole team of girls, some of whom barely knew me, who were shouting my name to encourage me. I would never participate in the real Olympics, but I can understand the sense of pride in winning for your team.

There were days when I really missed my home, a hot shower, a blue pool (without leeches), and my family and friends. I was very happy when my instructor called my name to say I had mail. A beautiful letter from Mom written on beautiful paper, a funny Hallmark card from Dad, or a letter from my two best friends.

On August 16, as I was hurrying to change for an activity, I heard young girls crying. I felt like something big had just happened. That's when a camper rushed at me: "Elizabeth, did you hear?"

"No, what?"

"Elvis is dead."

Was it a joke? I didn't believe her. That was not possible. He was always everywhere: on TV, in movies, in shows, in magazines. He was larger than life. I just couldn't believe it. I was overcome with sadness.

The month came to an end. My friends wrote me messages on pieces of paper. When my family picked me up, I jumped into their arms. We talked all along the car ride, with me telling them about my summer, and them filling me in on what I had missed. I was happy to get back to my house, my friends, my routine.

Thanks to this camp and my parents' decision to send me there, a certain part of me was transformed. Yes, I learned English, which I still use today, but I learned so much more. The distance makes us appreciate many things. The biggest lesson I learned was that I could survive alone without my parents, without my sisters, without everything that was familiar to me. A little trip in a cabin in the middle of the forest quickly made me realize how lucky I was to have a toilet and a hot shower at home. I had achieved everything I set my mind to. I didn't get eaten by a barracuda. I didn't miss big celebrations at home. I should never have wasted time worrying and being sad.

Now I've grown up and became a parent. But deep down, I'm still this child, because every summer I want to relive the summer of 1977 and its experiences, by jumping into a lake, singing loudly John Denver, eating s'mores by a campfire, sleeping in a cabin in the middle of the forest, playing games, having lunch with a good peanut butter and jam sandwich, doing arts and craft... Just playing outside and living in the forest with a gang of friends!

Yes, the camp made me appreciate nature and happiness in simplicity. But I learned something else too.

I learned that I could survive away from my comfort zone without being replaced, without missing anything. I learned that I could leave and then come back as a better person. So one day, I left for Lowestoft, and then for Barcelona, and for other destinations, other adventures... Alone.

Now, our childhood home is gone, and so are my parents. My original comfort zone has given way to a new one. I have transformed myself and... I survived!

Life is made up of change. We adapt, make adjustments, build ourselves, and shift our perspective. Long live the departures! Even if we are afraid, we go for it!

This is an important lesson to learn when you are young, and I'm glad my parents gave me that opportunity. It's not easy to let your kids go off on adventures away from you, but it's necessary.

When we arrived at the camp, my father stayed in the car while my mother went around the camp with me. In my young mind, I did not understand why my father did not come with us. He said goodbye to me very quickly.

My father was a protective man, very sensitive when it came to his daughters. When he stayed in the car, I interpreted it as coldness on his part. I jumped to the wrong conclusions: he is a man; a father can sometimes be unfeeling. That was the image of a man back then. Yet it was quite the opposite. As I got older and became a parent myself, I understood that he had to take refuge in the car precisely to let me go.

My mother, who was the typical housewife of her time, was considered fragile, yet in these moments she was the stronger one, even if deep down she was also very emotional, but it was necessary to "keep face" as they said.

Sometimes we misinterpret people's behaviour. We don't know what goes on inside their heads. Someone who appears to be cold may actually be crying a river inside. People express their emotions in many different ways. Strength and detachment can sometimes be veils for vulnerability and attachment.

PENNY FOR YOUR THOUGHTS

Is there anything your parents did as a kid that you didn't like, and that you can only appreciate and understand now, with hindsight? Do you remember a time when you faked being strong even though you were broken inside? What happy memory do you have from staying a few days in nature? What memories do you have from summer camp?

CHAPTER 11

LOWESTOFT: BREAKING OUT OF MY COMFORT ZONE

It's a funny thing about coming home. Looks the same, smells the same, feels the same. You'll realize what's changed is you.

—F. SCOTT FITZGERALD

PLAYLIST

Je vole · LOUANE
Could You Be Loved · BOB MARLEY
Let My Love Open the Door · PETE TOWNSHEND
Call Me · BLONDIE
Last Train to London · ELECTRIC LIGHT ORCHESTRA
Englishman in New York · STING
Don't Stand So Close to Me · THE POLICE
Ashes to Ashes · DAVID BOWIE
Another One Bites the Dust · QUEEN
Games Without Frontiers · PETER GABRIEL
All Out of Love · AIR SUPPLY
Whip it · DEVO
Shining Star · THE MANHATTANS
Celebration · KOOL & THE GANG
Late in the Evening · PAUL SIMON
Into the Night · BENNY MARDONES
Xanadu · OLIVIA NEWTON-JOHN
Hey Nineteen · STEELY DAN
Rapper's Delight · THE SUGARHILL GANG
Hello · LIONEL RITCHIE

On a Friday night, as I was watching one of my favourite series on Netflix, the British show *Sex Education*, my husband noticed an interesting detail in the show: a bus driving by, with its destination reading "Lowestoft." I was suddenly invaded by happy flashbacks from a long long time ago.

June 1980. I had just finished school, and my father had planned to send me to England. I had to fly on June 26. I had no desire to do so. My parents decided this for me. But what I really wanted to do was to stay at home all summer and see my friends, my gang. I was afraid of missing the best parties. In addition, I was going out with Will. How would I leave him behind?

This was another decision from my father to help me learn English, ever since I told him I wanted to go into business. When I called his office, his secretary Mrs. Dagenais answered in English to have a chat with me. I found it a little weird, but then again, his previous secretary did the same thing. My father looked for every opportunity to teach us. On the drive up to our cottage in the north, he started contests with my sister and me to see which one of us would speak English the longest. Sometimes we earned a quarter, sometimes a dollar. I know that these days, that sounds like hardly any money, but for a little girl like me it meant twenty five one-cent sweets. I loved it when my sister's friend Lelebeth rode with us, except when Dad started the English contest, because Lelebeth was perfectly bilingual, so whenever she was in the car, she was sure to always win the money prize. Sometimes she gave me a chance, and I got a dime! Ten cents worth of sweets is better than nothing. I would complement it by adding whatever I could find in my piggy bank.

During the war, Dad had to live in England for three years. He told me about it many times. The English were very fond of young Canadians. Dad found a language school in Lowestoft in Suffolk. Lowestoft is the easternmost city in Britain, the first place to see the rising sun. Other than to improve my English, I think another reason he wanted to send me to England was so he could relive a part of his youth vicariously through me.

June 24. I was leaving in two days. I packed my bags. I was happy when my friends came over and interrupted me. Marie-Jo, who adored David Bowie, asked me to get his autograph for her if I saw him. (There was very little chance that I would ever run into David Bowie in Lowestoft—ah the sweet innocence of youth!) She looked more excited than I was about my trip.

Sarah asked me to talk to her privately. Curious, I accepted, and we headed to the end of the field. I wondered why she wanted to go so far. She asked me if I was still dating Will. I said yes. She gave me a whole speech about how it was selfish of me. How could that be selfish? I did not really understand. She explained that I would meet some boys. I told her that it was a possibility, but that my heart was with Will. She said, "But what if *he* wants to date someone, and you end up meeting someone there?!"

Sarah got into my head, getting me confused and sad. I

didn't want Will to feel like a prisoner. So I decided to break up with him and say goodbye. He didn't understand and I had trouble explaining it to him, but I loved him too much to be selfish. So, I listened to Sarah's advice without telling Will that it was coming from her.

June 26. The big day! My parents left me at the airport. I flew with about fifteen teenagers I didn't know. After a seven-hour plane ride, we landed in Great Britain. I felt like I was being transported back in time to the post-war period. There was a strong energy in the air. Was it the fact that it always rained? Or was it their monuments which were much older than ours? The fact that they were not in a hurry to replace the old with the new? In England, they respect traditions, whereas in North America we are often prone to destroying old buildings and erasing the past. We want the new, always the new, as if we did not take the time to appreciate what we have. New is always better. But it all comes at the expense of history, of the soul!

Here we were in Lowestoft. I got off the bus. A lady with gray hair was waiting for me. This was my family for the next month. It wasn't a very large family, only a mother living with her son, the father having passed away some time before. Once we got to the house, my hostess showed me my room. I put my things there. I got ready for dinner. At dinner, I would also meet her son Graham, who was three years older than me. Graham turned the TV towards the table; I got introduced to Wimbledon. On my plate, I found spaghetti, beans, and salad. Dressing and sauce mingled together. For dessert, it would be biscuits and tea. We discussed our respective countries, my father who had lived in London during the war, the difference in our English expressions, leading to a discussion about the American "cookie" versus the British "biscuit." Finally, an English word that sounds like French!

It rained almost every day. Everything around me looked austere. I walked the dog in the evening, and everyone was running home to get warm; they didn't smile much... Well, except for the men coming out of the pub; they looked quite happy! I missed my home a lot. My comfort, my mother's good food, my father's old jokes, my sisters, my friends, my pets, our North American way of life. I wondered how I would survive! (Things are always more dramatic in a young girl's mind!)

I went to school in the morning by bicycle with my little map so I didn't get lost. In the afternoon I had horse riding lessons in the rain. It was cold and wet. My little pleasure was my chocolate bar at lunchtime, my Cadbury Fruit and Nut.

One night, at three o'clock in the morning, the phone rang. I heard Graham shouting angrily, "Elizabeth, telephooone!" I ran into the lobby to take the phone. I got scared that it could be bad news from my family. Nervous, I said, "Hello?"

And in amazement, I heard the sound of a young teenager's voice, "Elizabeth? How are you doing?" It was my best friend Cath.

"I'm okay, but what's going on?"

"Nothing," she said, "we just wanted to talk to you. Why?"

After a short, perplexed silence, I answered, "Oh nothing, just that it's three o'clock in the morning here!"

"Oops, we forgot about the time difference! It's 9 p.m. here," she said laughing. "I'll pass the phone to Marie-Josée!"

"Have you seen David Bowie?" Marie-Jo asked right away.

They told me everything that was going on back home, all the gossip, all the parties... Proof that life went on without me, so much so that Sarah was now dating Will... I went back to bed, happy to have spoken to them, but sad to be on the other side of the ocean, and sad to think that Will quickly forgot about me.

On a Saturday, Graham invited me to see the boat races on the waterfront—cigarette boats that went at a terrifying speed. The whole community was there for this yearly tradition. We walked together, discussed the differences between Anglophone and Francophone Canadians. We talked, we laughed. He studied science and was hesitating between pure science and agronomy for his future. I dreamed of being a diplomat. He was really nice. We got along well. In the evening, we watched a horror movie. There were only three TV channels. It was a far cry from the hundreds of TV channels we can choose from these days! He hesitated to put on a 1960 British horror film called *The Hand*. He thought that, being a girl, I was going to be very scared. But I'd already seen *Jaws*, *Alien*, *The Exorcist*, *Halloween*, *Carrie*... Poor Graham, he didn't know I was a horror movie buff! And let's just say that cinema evolved tremendously between 1960 and 1980.

I had a great evening. I already felt a little more at home, but I was still missing something.

One day the tide turned. It was lunchtime. The weather was nice, so we ate outside. I talked to other Quebeckers, and I got approached by funny French students who absolutely could not understand English. In the evening, they invited me to a small disco bar on the beach, the Pebbles. I loved it! From that moment, it became my favourite hangout. I spent my evenings dancing to Bob Marley's "Could You Be Loved," Blondie's "Call me," Pete Townshend's "Let my Love Open the Door"… That's where I met Serge. We had so much fun: we sang, we danced, and through the English lyrics I heard the strong French accents butchering the English words without knowing it. It made me laugh. Before going home, we sat on the beach to look at the sea. We talked, we laughed. It was beautiful. I was happy to be there. For a few moments, I forgot that I had not always been there.

After a few days a new resident arrived at our house, Jean-Claude. I liked him very much, and he was really nice. He was three years older than me and became my adoptive big brother who protected me. In the evening, we went out together to the Pebbles, and we came back together. He was careful never to let me go home alone. It was very dark on the streets of Lowestoft. When I was alone, I rode my bike at the speed of light, looking all around me, letting my imagination run wild.

I fell in love with Lowestoft and with Serge! At the end of the trip, our whole group of Quebeckers had to return to London. I remember crying big tears when it was time to leave, as if it was the end of the world. Serge would give me the scarf that he often wore, a trademark of the French. I would wear it every day in his honour until the end of the trip.

Once in London, we went to discover the city. I got to know my little travel group. Each person had their own style. One stood out to me in particular: Anne-Marie, our punk friend who originally gave me the heebie jeebies with her leather jacket, her chains, the green lock on her blonde and black hair, and her eyes always made up in black. She definitely looked very dark, but she was of unparalleled kindness. She convinced us to go see a punk show. At the end of the show, the singer threw bananas into the audience with "Buy my album" written on them. An original concept that I would remember for the rest of my life!

In the end, I met some lovely people during my vacation. Graham and his mother, Jean-Claude and his friends, Serge and all my Quebec friends.

It was hard to leave after a month. Strange how for a moment we wonder how we will survive, and finally we adapt, and we want to stay!

The hardest part was leaving Jean-Claude and Serge. I consoled myself thinking that one day we might see each other again in France. Having an older brother has always been a dream. I got along so well with Jean-Claude. Serge had become a boyfriend, and is there anything more magical than a summer love?

Serge and I wrote to each other for a year, and then one day nothing. Life took over. Same thing with Graham.

Jean-Claude was funny and brilliant. We wrote to each other for a year with the promise of seeing each other again. One day, I received a letter from his address, but I did not recognize his handwriting. I opened the envelope and read the letter. It was his mother. There was a picture of him. He had told me about his moped that gave him so much freedom. His mother wrote to me to tell me that I would not hear from him again. He had a tragic accident with his moped. He was her only son. Poor woman. I cried. I just couldn't believe it. He looked so alive, so happy in that picture. I responded to his parents. I tried to find the right words. I kept in touch for a while, and then life also just took over. Life is a funny thing sometimes.

I'm glad my father didn't listen to me. I am glad I made this trip. The goal was to improve my English, but I came back having learned so many other things.

For me, the success of a trip depends on the people. The people you meet make all the difference. The discussions, the contrasts, the discoveries…

I learned that you can lose your life when you are young and yearning for freedom. I learned to fend for myself, away from family, from friends, from everything that was familiar to me. I learned that I was lucky to have a family, sisters, parents. That it can be cold, rainy, and wet, and that you can still be in a good mood. Being far away from everything that is familiar to us has a way of increasing our self-confidence.

I often want to stay in my comfort zone. But I learned much more and grew up so much by being away from home, separated by an ocean, in an environment I hadn't chosen.

My father had sent me to the camp in New York and now in England, at this place where forty years earlier, he had been separated from his family for three years to serve in the war. I think he sent me there so that I could learn English, but maybe also unconsciously so that I could have a little taste of what it's like to take care of myself.

My father was very sensitive despite his strong appearance that would claim otherwise. At the airport, I had heard his voice trembling when usually it was so firm. He was sad to see me leave to go so far away, but he knew that the days were numbered before I would fly on my own, and he used all the possible lessons so that when that day arrived, I would be strong.

When you are a parent, you want to keep your children very close to you, but the mission of a parent is to prepare them for adult life, to put everything in place so that when they grow up, they can become independent. This involves the most difficult thing: letting them go. That's what they did that summer.

TTFN.[6]

---

6. "Ta ta for now." An expression my father picked up from a British radio show from his stay there.

PENNY FOR YOUR THOUGHTS

Do you remember the first time you came out of your comfort zone and started fending for yourself? How did it make you feel? What did you get out of it? Have you ever had that feeling of being an outsider when you first arrive at your travelling destination, but after a few days you feel at home?

CHAPTER 12

THE INTERNATIONAL ANGELS OF BARCELONA

Travelling leaves you speechless at first, before turning you into a storyteller.

—Ibn Battuta

PLAYLIST

Lindberg • ROBERT CHARLEBOIS
Variations sur le même t'aime • VANESSA PARADIS
Dis lui toi que je t'aime • VANESSA PARADIS
Crazy • SEAL
Hijo de la luna • MECANO
Kingston Town • UB40
Hélène • ROCH VOISINE
Papa Don't Preach • MADONNA
Si j'étais un homme • DIANE TELL
Don't Give Up • PETER GABRIEL
Invisible Touch • GENESIS
Pour une biguine avec toi • MARC LAVOINE
Maman a tort • MYLÈNE FARMER
Nothing Compares 2 U • SINÉAD O'CONNOR
She Drives Me Crazy • FINE YOUNG CANNIBALS
Chacun fait (c'qui lui plait) • CHAGRIN D'AMOUR
Week-end à Rome • ÉTIENNE DAHO
Roxanne • THE POLICE
Freedom! • GEORGE MICHAEL
Footloose • KENNY LOGGINS
Ghostbusters • RAY PARKER JR.
Missing You • JOHN WAITE
Oh Girl • PAUL YOUNG
I'll Be Your Baby Tonight • ROBERT PALMER AND UB40
Close to You • MAXI PRIEST
The Best • TINA TURNER
Safety Dance • MEN WITHOUT HATS
Closer Together • THE BOX
Pied de poule • GENEVIÈVE LAPOINTE

One summer as a young adult, I left for Europe, alone with my backpack. I was sad to leave everything I knew, my family, home, friends, and everyday routine… My comfort zone!

I knew that I was starting a new chapter. No longer a kid, I felt the independent woman emerging. If anything happened, I was on my own. Everybody else was on the other side of the ocean. If I needed rescuing, I had only myself to count on. The concept was scary, but the need for adventure was too strong to ignore. This would be a formative experience in my life.

I arrived in Barcelona, dreaming of becoming trilingual. So I took classes at a renowned international language school. My teachers were great and passionate. One of them liked to teach us Spanish through songs, and made us discover "Hijo de la luna" by Mecano. I fell in love with that song. Years later, I would listen to it, and I would be transported back to that time in Barcelona. If you want someone to learn your language, make them listen to music in that language. It's the best way.

In school, I made three good friends, an Italian, a Belgian-Portuguese, and an American from California.

I had an amazing time discovering Spain, the food, the people, the nature, the cafés, the restaurants, life… Travelling can be paradise, but everything can change in a minute. That's the way life goes.

I stayed with a Spanish family with another tenant, Javier,

a very nice guy from Porto, Portugal. He told me he had to get away from his hometown because of his drug addiction. He had been clean for seven months and was looking for a new start. I knew nothing about drugs and never felt an attraction to them. I had a good friend I loved, Olivia, who became addicted to cocaine after the death of her mother. Strangely enough, like Javier, Olivia had also been clean for the past seven months. She had driven me to the airport with my parents. She had confided in me that it was very difficult, like a seven-month itch. At the airport I asked her to stay strong and not to do anything stupid while I was away. When I met Javier, I felt that by helping him, in a strange way, I was also helping Olivia.

I went to school every morning. I felt like I wasn't learning Spanish fast enough. So Javier promised me that on that Saturday he would take me to spend the day with his Spanish friends so I could practice, and at the end of the day I'd be trilingual! We laughed. We helped each other a lot. He confided in me, and in return, he helped me with my homework when I needed it. Both away from home, we had started a nice little friendship.

One morning, I was waiting for the shower. I knocked and knocked but no answer. I got really worried, so I went through the window to find him on the floor. I tried to revive him. I ran to find a doctor next door. It was too late. We found Javier had a needle in his arm, hidden under his body. He had over-dosed. He was dead.

The adventure was no longer a happy one. The lady I lived with begged me not to tell anyone. It would be bad for her reputation. So I went to school as usual. Except nothing was " as usual." I felt like a walking zombie. I kept wondering, "Where is Javier now? Why didn't my gut wake me up earlier? Did he come knocking on my door for help and I did not hear him? What if I could have stopped it? What's the meaning of life? Why is this happening?..." I wanted to scream! I called my parents to make sure they were okay. I needed to hear their voices. Of course, I couldn't tell them anything. They would have had a heart attack on the spot! But I needed to make sure they were okay, and that Olivia was okay too.

My body went to school, but my mind was not there, as though it was in a different zone. The happy energetic kid I used to be was now transformed. Everybody was asking, "Are you okay?"

My only respite was the music I listened to. In the subway, I escaped with "Dis lui toi que je t'aime" by Vanessa Paradis, and temporarily, I was transported to a different world. I didn't feel so alone. Vanessa was with me and so was the friend who gave me this tape. I could escape reality for a little while. But reality always came back.

I felt like I stepped from paradise into hell in twenty-four hours. You know the saying, "one day at a time." It's so true, because twenty-four hours later, everything was going to change again. Like I said before, that's just how life goes.

That day, I couldn't speak for several hours, up until a point when I found myself alone with my three friends. I exploded! I couldn't handle it anymore. I was going crazy. Through my breakdown, I saw their mouths drop. I felt relieved. I was not alone anymore. Isabelle, my Belgian-Portuguese friend, exclaimed, "Enough with Barcelona! You are coming to my house. Get your bags. We are leaving. You are coming home with me. We are going to Belgium and Portugal!"

So we left. Isabelle and her parents empathized with my situation, so they pampered me. They introduced me to their friends. I got all these offers of people wanting to show me around their city, first in Belgium and then in Portugal. I saw beautiful places, biking in Holland for historic tours with Isabelle and her friends, jumping from a rock into the beautiful emerald ocean of Algarve in the south of Portugal, picking lemons in the garden one day with Monique, Isabelle's mom, picking almonds another day with José, her dad. I was back in paradise… Until it was time to leave. I fell in love with that family and that part of the world. Isabelle really was a godsend!

A few years later, I went to Isabelle's wedding. She came to mine with her mom. I went back with my husband and my son. Her younger cousin Justine came to study in Montreal, and I have bonded with her and her parents in Paris.

Today, with the pandemic, we can't go away on vacations, but my mind travels every time I come across Isabelle's Instagram posts of her surfing in the Algarve!

Why am I telling you this story? I don't know. Maybe because I needed to revisit happy memories in my mind, escape to better times?

Maybe I wanted to tell you to never give up if something bad happens. Keep believing because life works in mysterious ways. It really does. Maybe I wanted to tell you to be good to other people, because twenty years from now you could have a great friendship that started right about now! Or maybe I just wanted to thank Isabelle for taking me away from Barcelona that day, and taking me to her world!

Wherever you are, stay safe, and don't give up! You are not alone. A friendly hand could be just around the corner.

PENNY FOR YOUR THOUGHTS

Have you ever had a blessing come out of a tragedy? Did you ever have your life change from paradise to hell, or the other way around? What did you learn from that experience? Have you ever bonded with people on a trip, and you are now international friends?

CHAPTER 13

FRIENDSHIP HAS NO AGE LIMIT

Everyone has a friend during each stage of life. But only lucky ones have the same friend in all stages of life.

—ANONYMOUS

PLAYLIST

Un ami · NICOLA CICCONE
Young At Heart · FRANK SINATRA
It Was a Very Good Year · FRANK SINATRA
Witchcraft · FRANK SINATRA
Que Sera, Sera · DORIS DAY
The Girl from Ipanema · STAN GETZ AND JOÃO GILBERTO
Downtown · PETULA CLARK
I Got You (I Feel Good) · JAMES BROWN
C'est le temps des vacances · PIERRE LALONDE
Voir un ami pleurer · JACQUES BREL
You've Got a Friend · CAROLE KING AND JAMES TAYLOR
Stand By Me · BEN E. KING

Summer 1971. It was a beautiful, hot, sunny Saturday. I came back from playing at my friend's house at full speed on my banana bike. I was excited because Mom and Dad's best friends were coming over for a barbecue that night. We called them our uncles and aunts although they weren't actually blood relatives, but it seemed that they had become family nonetheless. They had seen us grow up. As a matter of fact, the first thing they told me when I saw them was often, "My God, how you have grown!" I never knew what to answer, but deep inside I was always happy to hear it.

I was home. I dropped my bike on the grass. I ran to the terrace in our backyard. I heard loud voices and laughter. It was Jack, our favourite uncle and my sister's godfather. Lucky her! She hit the jackpot! He spoiled her. Carole and I were jealous because our godfathers did not seem to know we existed! Fortunately, Uncle Jack adopted us all momentarily, each time he came.

He was a tall, handsome man with broad shoulders, piercing blue eyes, salt and pepper hair—a born charmer. He was a pilot in the army and a prisoner of war. He was a childhood friend of Dad's, and they lived a hundred tales together. When he was in the same room as Dad, I had the impression that my father, a serious fifty-year-old man, suddenly became a playful twelve-year-old boy.

When my parents' friends visited, it was like happiness

took over the whole house.

I said hi to everyone, starting with Uncle Georges. He was the quietest of them all, a good man. He did not show it, but he was a tough man, a prisoner of war for five years, a cancer survivor at forty-four. He had been through a lot. He had also met Frank Sinatra through his work! He was the father of my best friend whom I secretly loved, Michel. He was there, but I had yet to find him. I went to kiss his mom, Aunt Denise, a beautiful woman. She reminded me of Doris Day. She had the same short sexy blond hair but with big brown eyes instead of blue. She was a little like an adoptive mom to me, since I stayed at her house a lot. She always said I was her adoptive daughter since she only had a son. Aunt Denise was dedicated to her husband's health. I do not know if he would be alive if she was not there.

Then I said hello to Aunt Jocelyne, a strong headed and intelligent woman. She had been a nurse, a flight attendant, and at that point, she was in business with her husband Jack. She was a tough cookie, very straightforward, no bullshit. That's why we loved her, and that is exactly why Uncle Jack fell in love with her!

I finished answering Aunt Jocelyne's questions about school. I turned around, and I found Michel, right in front of Uncle Jack—where else? I was excited. I said hi to both, but they were busy. My two sisters were there too. Uncle Jack was performing a magic trick. All the kids were paying attention. He made a two-dollar coin disappear. Just when we were all wondering where it went, he made it come out of Michel's ear. We laughed! Then he performed another trick, and another.

For the big finale, he had brown paper bags full of goodies for each kid. Happy to be our star, he returned to the world of adults. Michel and I were ecstatic. We ran to the sofa by the pool to see what was inside our bags. We found a plethora of candy: Caramilk, Oh Henry, Malted Milk, Cherry Blossom, Crunchie, Bazooka gum… We started chewing while we read the little cartoons and exchanged jokes. We looked further in our bags and found colourful little plastic water guns. We started filling them up with water and then war broke out! We had so much fun.

Mom needed tomatoes for her recipe. Uncle Jack offered to get them, but only if we could ride with him to the store. How could we say no? On top of that, he had a brand new convertible. We happily jumped in the car. The sunroof was down, our hair was running in every direction with the wind, and we were smiling from ear to ear. What a wonderful feeling of freedom! If he asked us, we would never go back. We would continue to ride all day long. But Mom needed her tomatoes!

We jumped out of the car with Uncle Jack. Aunt Denise was in the swimming pool. She was a courageous woman: the water was freezing cold. Dad had stopped heating the pool, because he said we didn't swim enough. We joined her. We played Marco Polo for a while. Suddenly we were called for dinner. We jumped out of the pool, got dry, and ran to the table. While we were gone, more aunts and uncles had arrived. Aunt Suzanne was tall and beautiful, elegant like an actress, a Rita Hayworth type. Her husband Noel was an epicurean. He must have been a chef in another life because his cooking was amazing. He had a great sense of curiosity. He always knew about the latest gadgets. He introduced us to the microwave, and a decade later, he would introduce us to the CD player.

Food was almost ready. Time to get to the table, which was set up outside. The women sat first. Dad and the boys chatted over the barbecue, exchanging steak secrets, and joined us. Mom came out of the kitchen with more delicious food. All fourteen of us ate around the big round wooden table with the huge built-in umbrella over our heads. We watched the sunset over the water and listened to the different stories of our aunts and uncles' younger days. It started raining, and we laughed, feeling lucky we were witnessing the beauty of a wonderful summer evening together, just like a family.

We had many evenings like this. My aunts and uncles witnessed me getting older, and I witnessed them getting wiser. Even as a twenty-year-old, I loved spending evenings with them. Those were some of the best times in my life. Simple but perfect times.

As you get older, life throws you curveballs. We witnessed many of my uncles getting sick and dying. Our gatherings were different. Our conversations got deeper. My aunts dropped a few words of wisdom to me for whatever challenges I was going through while I listened to the stories of their younger days.

As a kid I thought Aunt Jocelyne was a little strict. I guess opposites attract. She sort of had to be because Uncle Jack was such a kid. We need balance in life. I got to know her and love her. I found out she was also young at heart but in a different way. She always had a new game to show us. Sometimes we played cards. Other times we played Ouija. We always had a blast. But at one point, she stopped playing Ouija, saying it was dangerous to play with the other side. She was ahead of her time: Before anyone else, she was the first to play bridge online with people across the globe.

She was a little responsible for my being with my husband. I remember telling her that I might not be going out with this man because I was afraid he was too young, to which she answered, "That is rubbish! Look at our generation! We married older men. They worked like dogs promising great later days. They got sick, we took care of them, and now they are all gone, so we live and travel alone! Your Martin sounds lovely. I say go for it. You think too much!" So go for it I did, and now we have been together for twenty-three years. And I have Aunt Jocelyne to thank for that.

Today, my parents and my adoptive aunts and uncles are all gone, except one: Aunt Denise, who is ninety-six years old. She moved twelve years ago to live in the same senior residence as Mom, but Mom left for a better world the week before my aunt moved. Tough blow.

Aunt Denise is my friend now. I pick her up when we have family celebrations, and she is so happy to be with us. We've had girls' nights at the cottage, drinking wine and laughing. Sometimes we just go for a car ride and chat. Sometimes I have to give her a pep talk at the hospital, so she knows that even though everyone is gone, there is still a younger generation of people who love her and are here for her.

She knew my parents when they were young. She saw me grow from a baby, a child, an adolescent, to a wife and mom. She even saw my son grow from being pea-sized to a six-foot-tall nineteen-year-old man. I love being with her and she loves being with me.

We lived two generations of friendship. We have a forty-year age difference, but most of the time, I just feel I am with my seventeen-year-old buddy sharing a very strong bond!

I wish we did not look at age so much when choosing friends. It is so amazing to chat with someone who has seen it all and can give you true pieces of wisdom.

Aunt Denise often jokes that God might have forgotten about her. If he did, I am glad. Being with her is comforting because she has known me for so long. Also, when I am with her, I see why my parents loved her, and I feel a little piece of them is still here. My egregore is alive and well!

PENNY FOR YOUR THOUGHTS

Did you grow up with people who felt like your second family? People who weren't related by blood, but felt just as close? What did they teach you? How did they help you grow? Do you have friends who are much older or younger than you? Do you have friends your kids love being around? Do you ever keep in touch with your parent's friends?

CHAPTER 14

MY CHOSEN FAMILY

*Friendship is the comfort of knowing that even when
you feel alone, you aren't.*

—ANONYMOUS

PLAYLIST

Grease • FRANKIE VALLI
Greased Lightnin' • JOHN TRAVOLTA AND JEFF CONAWAY
Back in Black • AC/DC
Suite Madame Blue • STYX
Say it Ain't So, Joe • MURRAY HEAD
Give a Little Bit • SUPERTRAMP
Your Song • ELTON JOHN
Ripples • GENESIS
Follow You, Follow Me • GENESIS
Stairway to Heaven • LED ZEPPELIN
Dream On • AEROSMITH
(I Can't Get No) Satisfaction • THE ROLLING STONES
Should I Stay or Should I Go • THE CLASH
Piano Man • BILLY JOEL
Under Pressure • QUEEN AND DAVID BOWIE
Africa • TOTO
Bicycle Race • QUEEN
Saturday Night • BAY CITY ROLLERS
Stayin' Alive • BEE GEES
Born to Be Alive • PATRICK HERNANDEZ
We Are Family • SISTER SLEDGE

I was five years old. My big sister was going to see her friend. She tried to sneak out, but Mom caught her right on time. Whether she liked it or not, she had to take me with her. We went to the Pelletiers' house. I rode behind her on her bike. I held on tight to her back, and I kept my feet way high in the air, so they didn't get caught up in the wheels. I loved it! She had to pedal, so she did not enjoy it as much! We got to our destination. She rang the doorbell. Her friend answered and called her little sister Nath. Nath arrived and the oldest siblings disappeared. The last thing they wanted was to spend time with their little sisters. We ran to Nath's room and played with Barbie dolls for a while. Nath was the youngest of a large family. I thought she was so lucky. We decided to go downstairs and watch her brother rehearse with his band. We thought it was so cool until her brother screamed, "Nath, get out of here!" Oh well, no free concert for us. We ran upstairs and were offered a piece of cake which we accepted gladly. We played a little more until my sister came for me: time to go home.

I was eight years old. Every morning, I took the bus to go to school. I had two new neighbours who were sisters. We waited for the bus, but we were too shy to talk. Then, one day my mom told me she spoke to them, and they would love to play with me. The next morning, I felt safe enough to talk to them. Bang! I just made two besties for life!

They lived in the house just in front of ours. We played together every day. Kick ball, basketball, tag, hide and seek, elastics, you name it, we played it. We dreamed of adventures. We dreamed of having a secret society. We grew up. We got interested in music and movies.

We were twelve years old. The movie *Grease* had just been released. We decided to go see it. We waited for the bus, got to the movies, sat in the theater, and fell in love with John Travolta. We wanted to sing all the songs. Before heading back home, we made a detour to the record store and bought the album. We hurried back to my house. I ran upstairs and carried my sister's record player outside on the patio. We sang our hearts out, we danced, we dreamed, and for an afternoon, we were Olivia Newton-John and John Travolta! Every time the movie plays on TV, I am transported in time and I am twelve years old again, singing, dancing, and laughing with my two buddies.

On Sundays, my friend Cath and I always got very excited. We took bets on who was going to be number one on *Casey's Top 40* every week. We both turned on our radios and stayed on the phone together, even though we were neighbours. Of course, my sisters found this a little annoying. Too bad, I was with my best friend and from ten to twelve, the radio and the phone were mine. My heart started beating when I heard the intro: "American Top 40, this is Casey Kasem in Hollywood, counting down the best songs in America! Let's get started!" We would then listen to the number-one song for weeks! We kept the tradition going for many, many Sundays. I guess today, some people keep it going with Ryan Seacrest!

I was fourteen years old. My besties and I had lots of fun together, but we were starting to think we would have even more fun if there were more of us. Riding our bikes, we bumped into a few boys and girls who used to go to the same school we did. We chatted and became friends. We rode our bikes to the corner store to get ice cream. We played football, basketball, and tennis. We went to the movies, listened to music, and started getting crushes on some of the boys. We gathered at the same spot every night. We called it the Attic, because it actually was the attic of a garage. We painted it. We installed a music system in it, a small carpet to sit on, and we signed our names, the ones we gave ourselves, on the wall to really make it ours. Somewhere on that same wall those names are still there—Mart the Pope, Liz Spagabeth…

I was fifteen years old, and it was Friday night. I ran to catch the train with Cath, Soph, Phil, Nick, Paul, Martin, Rick, and the whole gang. We were excited. Nick, who went to Collège Beaubois, bought us tickets for the dance held for Grades 11 and 12 in the school gymnasium. Everything was transformed to make way for a large number of teenagers. The DJ was on the second floor. It was dark, but not too dark. "Ballroom Blitz," "Under My Thumb" by the Rolling Stones, Queen, AC/DC… Rock was in the spotlight! Everyone danced or almost. Some just looked like they were jumping. When we were not dancing, we went around the room to see if there were friends we had not seen. Then, the volume of the music went down and changed pace. Couples got busy, getting closer together and flooding the dance floor. The girls crossed their fingers, hoping that a handsome boy would ask them to dance. Sometimes we got lucky. Sometimes we didn't. Sometimes we pretended to talk to friends to avoid being asked to dance. "Sweet Madame Blue" played, then Led Zeppelin's "Stairway to Heaven" and Murray Head's "Say It Ain't So, Joe." Sometimes my friend Paul came to rescue me. We danced, sang, and laughed. Nick waved at us. We had to run to catch the last train home!

At sixteen, we all got our driver's licences. We danced in more gymnasiums around the city of Montreal. At eighteen, we were finally dancing in downtown Montreal. Now I was interested in nightclubs. Not really for drinking, because my drug was really music and dance. I found myself at la Mansarde, DJ's, La Pleine Lune, 1234 rue de la Montagne (a former funeral home), Chez Swan... Madonna was often in the spotlight, so was Michael Jackson, the Police, Duran Duran, Van Halen, and so many others.

It seems my childhood friends and I were bound by music and our fun times playing together. Later on, our lives got busy, we got married, had kids, moved away, made new friends. We did not see each other often, but we talked on the phone, made sure that everyone was okay, and we caught up with each other.

On my birthdays, I invite them over, and we sing and dance. While eating amazing food, we reminisce about the good old days, just like I witnessed my parents doing with their friends. For the last twenty years, my friend Paul has been making me my favourite birthday cake: Baked Alaska Pie! It's the best gift!

My first friend ever was Nathalie. Of course, our activities have changed, but we still enjoy each other's company. Every

Monday night, I grab my computer, log on to Zoom, and I see her face on my screen and follow her meditation class. It is a very different beat from when we were five, fifteen, or twenty years old, but we still love to spend time together even after all these years have passed. Somewhere, somehow, we are still those two little five-year-olds having fun.

With our busy lives and the pandemic, we do not get to see each other as much as we would like, but when I play music, they are always on my mind, and I love them dearly.

When I hear Madonna, I think of Cath singing loudly and dancing.

When I hear AC/DC, I think of Paul, my best buddy with whom I danced at many parties and bars, having the best conversations on the way to the bar and back. I see him singing and dancing, off in his own little world.

When I hear Bowie, I think of Marie-Jo, calling me in England to ask if I have met him.

When I hear the Bee Gees, I think of Philippe and Nath in their first house before having three children. Just two young lovers on a Saturday night in their living room with me watching them, hoping that one day I would also get to live a great long-lasting love story.

When I hear Bread, I am in Lyzanne's basement where her father has set up a kind of home disco for her, thinking how lucky she is.

When I hear Genesis's "Follow You, Follow Me," I see Sophie, excited about making me discover this new song. Even though she now lives in the U.S., she remains close to my heart and one phone call away!

So many songs, so many great friends…

I have made new friends lately. It makes me wonder why we click with some people and not others, why we stay friends for life with some people and not others. I guess you need to share common interests and a similar sense of playfulness. You must be able to see the best in your friends. They must be there for you and you for them, in good times just as in hard times. In a way, just like when we fall in love with our life partners, we kind of have to fall in love with our friends too, don't we? It's another kind of love, just like loving a family member!

I hope you have good solid friends because in hard times they will make all the difference and become family.

PENNY FOR YOUR THOUGHTS

Have you made friends that you will keep through thick and thin? Maybe they are friends you don't talk to all the time, or don't get to see every day, but every time you see them, it feels like you never left their side? Do you remember how you met your oldest friends? Do you remember the games you used to play? The music you used to listen to?

CHAPTER 15

THE DOG CONNECTION

A dog is the only thing on earth that loves you more than he loves himself.

—JOSH BILLINGS

PLAYLIST

Belle · ZAZ
Belle et Sébastien · COEUR DE PIRATE
Who Let the Dogs Out · BAHA MEN
Dogs · PINK FLOYD
Dogs · DAMIEN RICE
I'll Name the Dogs · BLAKE SHELTON

REX, MY FATHER'S FIRST AND LAST DOG

1956. The Montreal Canadiens won the Stanley Cup. Elvis scandalized everyone with his swaying. The Quebecois singer Raymond Lévesque was singing "Quand les hommes vivront d'amour," which became an international hit. The Chevy Corvette became the iconic car of the year. Marilyn prepared a sexual revolution. Edith Piaf visited Quebec. My father got his first Polaroid camera and took pictures of everyone. Mom and Dad prepared their little nest.

My parents had just gotten married. They bought their first house and Mom was pregnant. My father was not a very tall man, maybe five foot eight or nine, but he dreamed of getting a tall dog. So he got a fawn Great Dane and called him Rex. They loved each other. He listened to my father to a tee, and my father was very proud of his dog!

One Saturday night, my father was outside on the terrace, making burgers on the barbecue with his friends all around him. He left the dog inside so as not to disturb the guests. He was telling his friends a story, gesticulating and raising his arms to heaven. Rex, thinking that my dad was motioning for him to "come here," rushed to his master, passing through the screen door to go sit in front of my father, showing what an obedient dog he was. Rex was happy to finally be invited to the party!

When you have a new home and no children, you have guests coming over more often. On another beautiful Saturday, the Tremblays, Champagnes, Poissants, and Thompsons came to dinner. My mother was busy in the kitchen. She wanted everything to be perfect while her friends begged her to come and have a drink in the living room with them. She took her roast beef out of the oven and put it on the counter to let it rest.[7] Once she was satisfied that everything was in order, she let out a sigh of relief, took off her apron, and rushed into the living room where she was served her glass of Cinzano, her favourite drink. The men were all drinking gin and tonic, and she could finally chat with her friends.

After a few minutes, she returned to the kitchen for a final preparation before serving. The first step was to cut the roast beef. She grabbed her electric knife, and turned around to find out that the roast beef seemed to have disappeared. Her stress level rose. She was sometimes known to be absent-minded, but this time, she was stumped. Where else could she have put the roast beef, other than the counter? With every passing second, her stress levels continued to spike. She thought she was going crazy for a moment.

And then she heard something. She turned around to see Rex licking his mouth and looking at her, his head at just the right height, that of the counter, looking at her as if to say, "Thank you, that was amaaaazing!" "Oh my God!" Mom exclaimed loudly. Her friends rushed into the kitchen to find her almost in tears. What would she serve for dinner? A roast beef for the dog and small triangle sandwiches for

---

7. See Recipes: Roast beef (p. 235)

the humans?! My parents' friends teased them for a long time, saying that in their next incarnation, they would want to come back as Rex! He had the good life!

A few months later, my eldest sister Carole was born. After the roast episode, one might wonder what Rex would do to Carole if he ever had a fit of jealousy. Mom and Dad had to make the difficult decision to say goodbye to Rex—one of the hardest goodbyes for my dad. He tried to find him the best foster home and ended up finding a chef! He told himself that Rex would have a good life and certainly good meals! Weeks went by. Curious, Dad decided to call the chef to get some news about Rex. The chef thanked him, saying he made a lot of money, because Rex was a pure breed, and he sold him! My father was speechless, rabid, and sad. His heart was broken. He would never touch or love another dog! He would forever remain true to his Rex!

THE DOGS OF MY CHILDHOOD

When I was six years old and my older sister was eleven, we watched *Belle et Sébastien* on TV together. Belle was a mountain dog from the Pyrenees and Sébastien was a beautiful boy. The show follows their adventures in the French Alps, where Belle, a large and intelligent dog, spends most of her time saving lives in the mountains.

Years later, I dreamed of getting a big smart dog. Every Saturday morning, I watched *George*, a Canadian-Swiss TV show about the adventures of a St. Bernard and his master in Switzerland. George was very funny because he was big and a little goofy. But mostly, he was intelligent, and spent his time saving lives. The St. Bernard, noted for his intelligence, strong sense of smell, and astute sense of direction, is known to save lives from avalanches and has become one of the emblematic dogs of Switzerland.

So I really wanted a big, intelligent, and protective dog. I told myself that one day I would have my St. Bernard! Through the years, we did have a few dogs—Napoleon, Josephine, Ponponnette, Prefix—but I dreamed of George…

When we got older still, my sister and I wanted a bigger dog, and my sister wanted to get a Husky Malamute, a breed very similar to a wolf. So we got Anouk! Anouk was much happier outside than inside. One time when I was fifteen years old, my parents went on a long trip, and my sisters weren't home. I was alone in the empty house, and I started to let my imagination get the best of me in the dark. But fortunately, I had Anouk sleeping in my room. A few times throughout the night, she would get up and make her rounds, like a wolf protecting her pack. I felt safe, knowing that Anouk would never let anyone hurt me, and I could sleep in peace.

When we went up to the cottage, she often escaped, but we would always find her leading a pack of friends. After a while, every one of the dogs in her pack went home, except one, who looked abandoned. We begged my mother to keep her, and she made a pact with us: if we went around the village and no one claimed her, the dog was ours.

Well, we did go through the village, and we eventually found the owners. But they had no interest in taking their dog back. My mom didn't expect that. But now, we had three dogs!

We decided to call her Sartre. The name was picked by my sister's boyfriend after he read a Sartre book. Our Sartre was a Borzoi, a Russian breed that looks like a greyhound. She had a caramel spot and the rest of her hair was a silvery white. She was a funny dog, but we loved her, and she became good friends with Anouk who had helped find her a loving family.

Sartre was able to smile on command, which was lovely. It felt like she understood us. During the summer, one of my joys was to take my bike, pedal at full speed while admiring Sartre, running gracefully and effortlessly at my side. She was such a beautiful sight, like a show just for me! I felt free as the wind and so did she.

One day as I came home from school, Anouk was not there to welcome me. The welcome-home parties she threw for me were always a highlight of my day. It's always good to see someone who's happy to see you. It's good for morale.

In general, if you leave a Husky Malamute free, they will go off and conquer Quebec, not waiting for you to call them. These dogs have no notion of time, and Anouk could leave five minutes or three days, it was all the same to her. But that night she wasn't there. She had escaped and ran out with joy to conquer the world. But a car had stopped this race forever.

My sister explained that Anouk had left for another world and would not return. She was only five years old. That night, I cried all the tears in my body, and the next morning when I went to school, I was still crying. When you go to a girl's school, there's a lot of gossip going on, and everyone wonders why you're crying. So my classmates asked me what was wrong, and I replied that my dog was dead.

That morning, my grief was the subject everyone talked about. Through this game of telephone, I found out it was easy for the truth to get distorted. Anouk was dead and I had no desire to go to class, so I took my time. When my teacher Miss Michaud took attendance and I wasn't there, the students explained that I had left for another world. You can imagine the cries of surprise I heard when I showed up at the door of the class, very obviously alive. "We thought you were dead!" my classmates and teacher told me. I burst into tears again, explaining through my sobs that it was my dog who died, not me!

A few months after Anouk's departure, my parents decided to go on a romantic trip, leaving Jo and me alone (what a mistake!). My oldest sister Carole had gotten married and moved out by then. Jo and I felt a void without Anouk there, so we looked at books with dogs in them. We wanted to get another really big dog—a Newfoundland. One day when I came back from school, I was pleasantly surprised to find a little Newfoundland puppy in our living room that Jo had gotten. I was so happy!

Jo showed me a picture of a huge dog, saying, "It will be that big when it's all grown up!" The dog in the picture looked like a big teddy bear and I was jumping with joy. But then I came back down to Earth and told her, "What about Mom and Dad? What will they say?"

"Let me worry about that!" said Jo. When Mom came home, the news about the dog put her on the verge of a nervous breakdown, despite our promise to get really good grades in school. Obviously, she didn't see it as we did. Instead, she thought of dog hair getting everywhere, training, cleaning… At the time, being two teenagers, we found her really negative. But obviously today, with hindsight, I can see where my mom was coming from.

For me, a moment of joy was when I jumped into the pool and heard another loud splash right behind me. Before I could turn around, I heard my mother shouting, "Not in the pooool!" And I realized that my big doggy had jumped in to save me. Newfoundlands are great swimmers, and they have the instinct of a lifesaver. Isn't nature amazing?

With every new dog, it seemed like I was closer and closer to my dream of getting a St. Bernard, although I didn't know it yet.

After moving out, when I was single, I still couldn't resist a beautiful dog. One time when I was having dessert on a patio with a friend, I exclaimed, "Oooh, he's gorgeouuuus!" My friend turned around looking for a handsome man, only to find out I was talking about a dog.

KAYLA

The years have passed. I got married. I had a child, and now it was my turn to have a dog. Someone told me that sometimes we get a pet to fill a void. I guess it's true. I was always hoping to have a second child, and my wish was not granted. So yes, Kayla did fill a void, but today she is part of the family. I wanted a dog but I didn't want to experience the loss of a dog. I thought to myself one day when I would have the courage to endure that loss, I would have a dog. It was somewhere in the back of my head and my husband's. My long list of criteria for a husband included, "Must love dogs." We agreed to only have the dog when the time was right.

One night, we saw *Marley & Me*, the true story of a journalist who was writing about his adventures with his dog. This film gave us hope and courage. At the end of the film, the author passes the message that it is difficult to lose a dog, but on the other hand they bring us so much. It was there, when we left this movie theater that we decided we were going to have a dog for the summer. It was January. We had time. I started looking but I could only find small dogs, and I wanted a big one who could play with my son and make sure he's safe, but not one who would scare our guests.

My friend Jonathan lives up north. If you're looking for something he will find it! He always amazes me. So I decided to call him and ask if he knew where I could get a dog for the summer, a Labrador mixed with a German shepherd or something else. To my surprise, he said yes! He would be at our cottage that afternoon with a dozen puppies. He came with twelve adorable Labernese puppies (a mix between Labrador and Bernese). I would have taken them all! But I fell in love with one in particular. She came to bite my fingers. It is said that dogs choose us, and she chose me, so we adopted her! I decided to call her Kayla, after Kay, King Arthur's favourite Knight of the Round Table.

The Labrador side of the Labernese is the one that always wants to play. The Bernese side is the Swiss origin making them real mountain dogs, really close to a St. Bernard, just like Belle and George! She loves to play frisbee and find cookies or hidden friends. She would have made a fantastic guide dog.

When my son was scared all alone in his room, she would lie down on the floor beside his bed. Feeling safe, he would fall asleep. He played with her outside in the snow. They played hide and seek, and Kayla found him every time. She learned a multitude of tricks in no time. She has a thirst for learning. If we leave her on her own outside, she waits for us. She calms my nerves and makes me feel good. I walk with her every morning. Thanks to her I am in good shape and in good spirits. Thanks to her I stop to look at the nature around me. She is a good teacher. We can learn a lot from dogs. Sometimes they help us understand ourselves.

Every morning when my son was little I drove him to school and I continued my way to the dog park around the corner. One day, I entered the park. Kayla ran in one direction to say hello to another dog. That day I noticed there was a weird energy in that park. I later learned that an aggressive dog had just left, but it felt like he left some kind of uneasy energy behind.

I'm never afraid of dogs, so I approached this golden doodle that I'd seen before, and he was usually very nice. I leaned down to pet him, but he started growling. It felt like he was going to bite me. It wasn't a good day for him, and I got the feeling that if I didn't back off, it would be a bad day for me too. So I just stood very still, invaded by fear. All of a sudden, Kayla arrived at full speed, circling around me to keep the other dog away. She kept her head held high, as if to say, "If you think you're going to attack my mistress, you've got another thing comin'! Back off!"

The other dog walked away. I was amazed by the instinctive intelligence that Kayla had just displayed. I didn't realize she had that in her. It was a nice lesson. I learned to follow my instincts when it comes to weird energies, and to just change direction. I also learned that mountain dogs make circles around the people they want to protect!

Labernese dogs are not aggressive dogs by nature. I was happy that she was nice but before that day, I couldn't help but wonder if she would be able to defend herself or others. That day, I got proof. Labernese dogs are kind of like dolphins. Dolphins are really nice creatures, but they can also kill a shark if it threatens them.

Another day, I was at the dog park with a friend who had just gotten a new Australian shepherd. He's a nice dog, and he and Kayla get along very well. Kayla is a little younger and a little more energetic. That day, her energy annoyed the Australian shepherd who decided to show Kayla who's boss. He ran after her and bit her tail as if to tell her to stop running so much. Kayla didn't think much of it at first. But then he bit her again. She still didn't say anything. But the third time, she stopped, turned around, grunted, got all big and bared her teeth at him, as if saying, "I'm nice, but don't push it!" The Australian shepherd looked surprised and became all sweet. All of a sudden, Kayla had become the boss.

This story showed me that sometimes you have to be nice, but other times you have to put your foot down if you want to be respected. When you do that, you'll often realize that the bully is actually just a big teddy bear.

In the period of stress that we live in, my husband has often told me that having Kayla resting at his feet during important meetings makes him feel good. And I feel the same way. She shows a presence and an intelligence that is very different from ours. She's like an anti-stress coach. It's good for morale and mental health. It's good for the head and the heart.

Life is a funny thing. In my childhood, I dreamed of having a dog like Belle or George. And Kayla is a perfect mix of the two. Is it just a funny coincidence? Or is it a perfect example of how the TV shows we watch as kids influence our decisions? Maybe my attraction to big dogs is just something I inherited from my dad.

When I think of what makes me happy in life, I think it's love—a family, good friends, a home, and a dog. Now Kayla will soon be thirteen years old, a little more tired than when she was young. But when I take her to the lake, and she runs to catch a stick, you would think she's only two years old. When I watch her, I feel a bit like a two-year-old myself!

PENNY FOR YOUR THOUGHTS

Do you have memories of a childhood pet that made your life a little better? What kinds of pets do you like? Do you have pets now? How did you choose them? What do they bring to your life?

CHAPTER 16

FOR BETTER AND FOR WORSE

Young lovers seek perfection. Old lovers learn the art of sewing shreds together and of seeing beauty in a multiplicity of patches.

—*HOW TO MAKE AN AMERICAN QUILT*

PLAYLIST

J't'aime tout court · NICOLA CICCONE
Une chance qu'on s'a · JEAN-PIERRE FERLAND
J't'aime pas j't'adore · NICOLA CICCONE
N'oublie jamais · RAYMOND BERTHIAUME
Ils s'aiment · DANIEL LAVOIE
Et si tu n'existais pas · JOE DASSIN
La maladie d'amour · MICHEL SARDOU
Pour vivre ensemble · CHANTAL PARY
Je l'aime à mourir · FRANCIS CABREL
Ma préférence · JULIEN CLERC
Je te promets · JOHNNY HALLYDAY
Hymne à l'amour · EDITH PIAF
Si t'étais là · LOUANE
Viens on s'aime · SLIMANE
La chanson des vieux amants · JACQUES BREL

Sometimes, when our parents leave us, we lose sight of family members. Yet this is the last thing we should do because many can inspire us for life.

2021. We were in the middle of a pandemic. She was eighty-seven years old. She witnessed her husband's stroke. She panicked. The paramedics arrived. They took him away. She could not go with him. Covid protocol. She had to leave him alone and wait alone to find out what was going on. These were the longest hours, days, of their lives. She had always been defined by her strength of character, but at this point she felt like a vulnerable child.

Sixty-five years of living together. They worked together, raised their children together, even fought cancer together. They had the most beautiful moments and grieved many times, hand in hand! They spent practically every night of their lives together. Then all of a sudden, a complete stranger decided their fate.

They met when they were both twenty years old. He worked in aviation. He came from a large family of ten children. She was a few months younger than him. She had seen and experienced some horrors. He most likely fell in love with her beauty and especially with her outspokenness. She fell in love with his piercing blue eyes, sense of humor, and quiet strength. Hard to resist a man in an aviator's uniform! They got married six months after their first meeting!

She fell in love with him and then with his family. They welcomed her with open arms. Rose-Marie and Gabriel, his parents, loved her very much, and she very much loved them back.

They got married. They had three beautiful boys of whom they were very proud. They even had grandchildren.

The phone rang. It was official: he had a stroke. Not easy to take the news. So many questions. Would he ever be independent again? Would he walk again? Talk? Recognize her? Come back home?

She went to visit him. It wasn't easy to go home alone and leave him behind, alone in his hospital bed. It wasn't easy to keep their distances and hear each other through masks and wearing what looks like a spaceman's suit. It wasn't easy to try to explain to young people that this gentleman was not an "old man," but an extraordinary man.

She had called him her boyfriend for sixty-five years. She never liked the word "husband"—too severe, too cold. It is true that if you didn't know them and you met them in a hospital room, you would jump to the conclusion that they were old, but in reality, they were still like two teenagers in love!

The years damaged them a little. They had wrinkles, white hair, but above all, they had sharp minds and extraordinary life wisdom. They could make you laugh out loud for a minute and give you the greatest life advice the next.

He had trouble walking and talking, but when he saw her enter his room, life came back to him. Strength returned to him. Love is a strong medicine.

She spoke with the doctors. They played the same broken record that they repeated to other patients of the same age, "You know, madam, you won't be able to take him home…" They tried to discourage her. They even told her that her husband would be moved at the end of the week to a ward from which he would never leave. Once in this ward, she would be allowed to visit him once a week with a mask and the spaceman suit. She was enraged!

She met with specialists, who can be impressive and make you insecure. Health is their domain. They have spent more time at university than anybody else. They are often given carte blanche, no questions asked. When we are faced with a bad diagnosis, we become overwhelmed with emotions and can't think straight. So we allow decisions to be made for us. We follow, like sheep.

But the specialists didn't know everything. They saw an eighty-seven-year-old and imagined an elderly and frail woman. But watch out! She would defend her other half like a lioness.

This broken record about old age, she wouldn't have it. She interrupted specialists, saying, "You take care of making him walk, and I will take care of giving him love and every-thing else, but at home!"

She gave a life lesson to each of these great specialists who all came out of it speechless, having learned something that a decade at the best of university cannot teach. Each person is unique, each person has a story that must be listened to, but above all, love is the strongest!

She won. She took her lover out of the hospital on a Friday. He did not walk as fast as before, but he was making progress every day. He was so happy to be in his house, on his sofa, and in the arms of his girl. That night, like every night, they would spoon each other to sleep and dream of their first dance. The following day at sunrise, things were not easy. It was quite an adaptation, but at eighty-seven years old, they had lived through many hard times, and above all, they were doing it together.

If you ever met them on the street, you would see their wrinkles, their gray hair, their slow walk, and you would think that they were fragile, but think again! Being strong is an inside job. Strength is in their head and in their hearts. They drew this strength from their youth and built it through the difficult years. This strength is love. Sixty-five years of love!

She's my aunt Yolande, and he's my uncle Claude, my mother's little brother. I love them. I am proud of my aunt, who imposed her values with conviction, for the love of her husband, in a healthcare world that often works mechanically, forgetting the human factor. She has shied away from nothing: neither from her fears, nor from so-called experts, nor from the difficulties that she faced. Perhaps we would have a better world if everyone had such strong values...

Long live the people who defy the status quo, and long live love!

Life is made up of choices, some more difficult than others. Surabhi Surendra once said, "A happy marriage is about three things: memories of togetherness, forgiveness of mistakes, and a promise to never give up on each other." Yolande and Claude know this more than anyone I know.

Don't let others dictate your life. Think of Yolande, go for it, and break down the doors and the rules, especially for the people you love. Yes, there are always more options than those presented to you. There is always a way to draw on your inner strength, even when you think you're all out.

In these difficult times, whether you are twenty or seventy, my hope is for you to open your heart. I hope you too have a boyfriend, a girlfriend, a friend, a brother, a sister, a cousin, a nephew, a neighbour... Someone who will fight tooth and nail, ready to move mountains out of love for you.

Sometimes our life lessons come from our parents. Sometimes they come from an uncle and an aunt!

Let's collect the human stories that bring healing to our heart and link us together.

PENNY FOR YOUR THOUGHTS

Is there a couple in your life who is a perfect model for a long and lasting marriage? A couple who is your inspiration for what a marriage should be? Two people who love each other in old age as much if not more than they did when they first met?

CHAPTER 17

SAYING GOODBYE TO MOM

You are no longer where you were, but you are everywhere that I am.

—Victor Hugo

PLAYLIST

C'est ma vie • ADAMO
Si Dieu existe • CLAUDE DUBOIS
Hier encore • CHARLES AZNAVOUR
Une enfant • CHARLES AZNAVOUR
Le temps • CHARLES AZNAVOUR
Le petit roi • JEAN-PIERRE FERLAND
Et maintenant • GILBERT BÉCAUD
Je reviens te chercher • GILBERT BÉCAUD
L'important c'est la rose • GILBERT BÉCAUD
Quand on n'a que l'amour • JACQUES BREL
La valse à mille temps • JACQUES BREL
Ma préférence • JULIEN CLERC
Non, je ne regrette rien • ÉDITH PIAF
L'été indien • JOE DASSIN
Chanson sur ma drôle de vie • VÉRONIQUE SANSON
Comment te dire adieu • FRANÇOISE HARDY
Frédéric • CLAUDE LÉVEILLÉE
Paroles, paroles • DALIDA AND ALAIN DELON
Sous le ciel de Paris • YVES MONTAND
Évidemment • FRANCE GALL
Une belle histoire • MICHEL FUGAIN
Je t'aimais, je t'aime, je t'aimerai • FRANCIS CABREL
Belle • DANIEL LAVOIE, GAROU, AND PATRICK FIORI
Mommy • PAULINE JULIEN
Il suffirait de presque rien • SERGE REGGIANI
Il suffirait de presque rien • ISABELLE BOULAY
Si jamais j'oublie • ZAZ
Ave Maria • CÉLINE DION

Friday, November 13, 2009. What a year! Michael Jackson and Farrah Fawcett, who had marked my adolescence, passed away. Obama fever was in full swing. But for me, it was one of the most challenging years of my life, for a completely different reason. Before I get there, let me tell you about my mother.

Gisèle had beautiful eyes—sometimes blue, sometimes green, sometimes gray, but always beautiful!

She loved children very much. Good for her, because much of her time was spent taking care of her siblings. Being the eldest, she had to set a good example and be responsible.

At the age of seventeen, she was tired of being the responsible one, so she left her parents' house. She wanted to be independent and be like her favourite aunt, a fashion designer. So she found a job as a seamstress.

In 1948, Gisèle was nineteen years old and dreamed of a man in uniform. The war had just ended, and Canadian soldiers were seen as superheroes. She met Jean, eleven years her senior. It was love at first sight, for both. She wanted to be the perfect housewife, so she took classes in diction, cooking, and everything to be the perfect housewife.

Six years later, Jean and Gisèle got married and had three daughters. My mom was fantastic. She had a beautiful *joie de vivre*. She liked to sing in the car—Aznavour, Bécaud, and Reggiani. She loved the piano, so her three girls learned the piano. She loved people and they loved her back.

She spent many hours on the phone with Madeleine, Florence, and many others. If anyone said something mean about an acquaintance, she quickly came to their defense. She was a good person.

Every night, she prepared a good dinner, because she found our family dinners important. Every morning for breakfast, all the boxes of cereal were laid out on a beautiful table with freshly squeezed orange juice. Sometimes even with a small note—"Good luck on your exam today!"

It was very important that her daughters be healthy, so she was one of the pioneers of buying brown bread and healthy cereals. If we were lucky (well, not really…), she made us a good healthy juice from her juicer with apple, carrot, and celery. Ah, and let's not forget about the big spoonful of cod liver oil to top off this healthy cocktail! (Ew!)

She had a heart of gold. She hosted her friends, our friends, and family… Everyone was always welcome.

For Halloween costume contests at school, she often spent nights making costumes for me. I was a bottle of 7 Up, a skunk (yeah, I know…), and Kermit the Frog, among others. Often, I could not win the contests, because her costumes were so well made that the judges believed they were rented! She probably would have been a great designer, but she chose to be our mother.

Gisèle was beautiful. She wore practically no makeup and never had a wrinkle. She was cute and feminine, often in a skirt or a dress, with small, elegant shoes.

She was always in excellent health. I don't know if it was because of the cod liver oil, the molasses, or the garlic that she put everywhere. Did I tell you that she was a wonderful cook?

She was nice, funny, and had an innocent look, but when she sat at the bridge table with her friends, she often surprised everyone by winning first place!

I loved her. That's why in 2009, I devoted all my time to her. It's not always easy when you have an eight-year-old child. It was important for me to paint her portrait, because when we think about an eighty-year-old lady, we often picture an unimportant elderly person. This is rarely the case. Older people are often young people trapped in an old body which does not reflect the youth in their hearts.

In 2008 and 2009, I moved my mother four times. I visited the hospital with her countless times. She had been diagnosed with Alzheimer's. As if that weren't enough, her breast cancer reappeared. I was burned out, exhausted, and so were my sisters. My heart was broken into a thousand pieces. The doctor gave her three to six months. I couldn't imagine not seeing her anymore. But I considered myself lucky to be able to be with her every day. I remained very strong in front of her, although I always imagined the worst. I always took a deep breath before entering the residence, and yet, believe it or not, even as she approached her death, I lived the purest moments with her. There was an extraordinary connection between us.

Often before she got sick, I'm sad to admit that I think I took her for granted. She had always been so healthy, with a pink glow in her little cheeks, that I thought she was definitely going to live to be ninety or a hundred years old. So I was often in a hurry, sometimes impatient, not present. But now that I knew her days were numbered, she had my full attention.

I was afraid to enter her apartment, but once I was there, I didn't want to leave her. Often, she slept in her room, and I stayed in the next room. I also often stayed close to her to write. I felt like I wasn't doing anything and yet time was passing by so fast. I wanted to stop time. One of the last times I was with her, I felt like I was with my child. I lay down next to her, holding her in my arms. She hardly spoke. That time, she said softly, "This feels good." It was a beautiful gift. Another time, we looked at each other, and I felt filled with love looking into her eyes. She gave me a beautiful smile and told me, "My Zabeth!" This was the nickname she gave me as a little girl. I felt like I was five years old again. An incredible feeling of love invaded me. She was there, Gisèle. She was there, my mother.

On Friday the Thirteenth, a few minutes before midnight, she passed away. She gave me everything, and in return I gave her everything I had. Our love did a 360. It went full circle.

I am writing this on Friday, November 13, 2020. My sister asked me if I was sad. The answer is no. Sure, I would have liked to keep my mother forever, but I know that this is not possible. It's the cycle of life. Over time, we understand and accept it.

We attach great importance to the last moments of life, but what matters is the legacy that a parent leaves us: the good memories, the small moments of happiness, the love we felt, the good meals we shared, the life lessons and values that we practice, and the traditions that we carry on with the next generation. This is what I call my egregore, that energy of love going full circle from one generation who wants the best for us to the next.

No, I'm not sad because I always feel her there. I start my day with her voice—"Don't forget your breakfast, it's the most important meal of the day!" And strangely, I find myself repeating it in turn to my son! All day long, I hear her voice.

It is still there. In my everyday routine, in my sisters, her sisters, my nephews, my son. In every meal I prepare, I see myself with her in her kitchen, happy at the idea of gathering everyone around her delicious dishes and her beautiful table.

No one ever really dies. We leave some of our energy behind. I do not understand everything, but I know that as long as there is love, we never die!

PENNY FOR YOUR THOUGHTS

What was the most authentic conversation you ever had with either one of your parents? A conversation where you truly felt like you had gotten to the heart of who they were? Are you ever impatient with your parents? Have you ever felt an energy of pure love coming over you when connecting to a family member?

CHAPTER 18

LIFE CYCLES

I will call to the past, far back to the beginning of time, and beg them to come and help me at the judgment. I will reach back and draw them into me, and they must come, for at this moment, I am the whole reason they have existed at all.

—*AMISTAD*, ABOUT ONE'S ANCESTORS

PLAYLIST

Je serai là pour toi · GINO QUILICO
Don't Blink · KENNY CHESNEY
I Hope You Dance · LEE ANN WOMACK
93 Million Miles · JASON MRAZ
Stand By Me · BEN E. KING
In My Life · THE BEATLES
Teach Your Children · CROSBY, STILLS, NASH & YOUNG
You're Beautiful · JAMES BLUNT
1973 · JAMES BLUNT
Take Me to Church · HOZIER
House of Gold · TWENTY ONE PILOTS
Superman (It's Not Easy) · FIVE FOR FIGHTING
Prendre un enfant · NANA MOUSKOURI AND YVES DUTEIL
L'escalier · PAUL PICHÉ
Hallelujah · LEONARD COHEN
Love Generation · BOB SINCLAR

Nineteen years ago in a few hours, at 3:08 a.m., I gave birth to my son. Incredible. I couldn't imagine anyone calling me Mom. I had been someone's daughter all my life, the sister, the friend, the girlfriend, Elizabeth, Zabeth, Babeth, but never Mom.

It seemed incredible to me, even if I wanted it with all my heart. I felt like I was going to jump into another dimension. I couldn't wait for this little thing to call me Mom. I couldn't wait for him to communicate with me. Yet, today, he has no problem communicating. "Mooooom, I am going out!" "Mooooom, where did you put my things?"... I really feel like my past is in another life. Even my son has a lot of trouble imagining that I have ever been anything other than his mother. And yet...

It's been almost twenty-three years since Martin and I have been together. We moved in together after our third date. It was love at first sight. After we got engaged, we decided it was time for the next step: a family. I got pregnant almost as soon as I thought about it!

We were very happy. I announced it to Martin by writing it on the bathroom mirror with red lipstick. We did not tell anyone at first. It was February. I lost the baby after a few weeks. I cried all the tears in my body. What if I never got to have children again? I felt so much anxiety! The doctor told me that the human body was well made. There must have been something wrong with the baby, so my body had taken care of it. He must have been right because on the next attempt, a few weeks later, I got pregnant again.

We waited three months before announcing it with a box containing two small baby shoes as a clue during a dinner in my family home, at the same table I'm writing this on right now! I was filled with happiness. I hesitated between two names, Christophe and Charles for Charles Aznavour. It ended up being Charles, a great joy for Grandma Gisèle who looooved Aznavour!

I loved being pregnant. I felt so good. There is something magical about creating a life, bringing it from the size of a pea to the complete formation of a human being. That is no laughing matter! My pregnancy itself was easy. What was happening around me, not so much.

One beautiful summer day, while I was shopping, I received an emergency call from my sisters: "Elizabeth, can you come over right now? Dad is not well. He is acting weird." I could hear panic in their voices. I rushed over. My dad, my Superman, my pillar! What was going on? I arrived on the terrace. My sisters explained to me that Dad could no longer open a door, no longer knew how the TV remote worked, or how to dial the phone.

Luckily, I got an emergency appointment with a neurologist. I rushed there with Dad. I didn't want him to suffer. I was answering all the questions for him until the doctor said to me, "Madam, let him answer. Hello, Mr. Péladeau, do you know what day it is?"

"No," said Dad.

"How old are you?"

My father smiled, happy to have the answer to that question. He looked at me, then looked at the doctor, and answered, "Fifty years old!" It was sad but funny at the same time, because my father was eighty-two years old. Overnight, he had gotten thirty years younger. The three of us burst out laughing. The stress went down. The doctor confirmed that Dad had a stroke. He was in good hands. We had to go to the hospital as soon as possible to give him treatment. Then I drove him back to his house. He was scheduled to begin his rehabilitation the next day.

On my drive home, through the Dorval tunnel, I began to cry. My father was a strong man. I was convinced that I would have him around until he was at least a hundred years old, another twenty years away. My father was a go-getter, a strong man, physically and mentally. But that day, I saw that he was not, in fact, Superman. This is what fathers often are in the eyes of their daughters. I was going to lose him. I could not imagine surviving this ordeal. I was crying and rubbing my belly, talking to my baby, telling him that I hoped that one day we would have the same strong bond. I felt lonely but thanks to him, I was not so alone.

Months passed. I received a call from the rehabilitation nurse who had me down as an emergency contact. She wanted me to talk to my father to tell him that he would not be able to play bridge or drive again.

My father refused to believe it. His mottos in life were, "Where there's a will, there's away," and "Decide, act, persist." My father was pig-headed, so if I told him he couldn't drive, he wouldn't listen to me. Why even bother trying to convince him? If it were true, he would see it for himself. Well, it turned out the nurse was wrong, and my father was right. Where there's a will, there's a way. And my father definitely had the will. He failed his driver's licence test on the first try. He went back and made it the second time. He was behind the wheel of his car and playing bridge again, despite a stroke, despite his eighty-two years of age. That was the kind of strong man my father was.

When my son was born in December, my husband took three weeks off. It was magical. We were in our own little world. Our days were spent eating, napping, breastfeeding (well my days were anyway), and admiring all of our baby's little gestures.

When January came around, it got more difficult. Martin went back to work. I was alone in the apartment with the baby, without any visitors. It was difficult to walk around the snow banks, in the cold. Martin left early in the morning and came home late at night, tired and burned out. The "baby vacation" was over.

I decided to go visit my parents in Florida. It was paradise—sunny and warm. My mother loved helping me with Charlie. She served me fruit plates which I ate while looking at the sea. I was spoiled. My mother rocked Charles back and forth with great happiness. I could breathe a little. My father did not hold my son. He was too afraid to drop him. But he looked at him for a long time. One day, I found him looking at him with a very thoughtful look, as if they were both talking to each other telepathically. I asked Dad what he was thinking, and he replied, "Life. I'm at the end of mine and Charlie is just starting his." My heart broke. I had a lump in my throat. I didn't know what to say.

Sometimes, during the day, I would drive Dad to his golf lessons. I stayed in the car with Charles and waited for him. I would watch him swing his clubs, hit his ball, and I would think to myself, "It's amazing how much I love this strong man, who always wants to move forward, who's always learning." And I felt overflowed with the love I had for my father and the love I had for my son right next to me. I hoped Charlie would be a bit like Dad when he grew up.

One day during that trip to Florida, Dad told me, "You know, life is a funny thing. There are cycles and chapters. One day you see friends, and you ask them, 'What school do you go to?' Later it's, 'Are you married?' Later it's, 'Do you have children?' Later still, it's, 'Are you retired?' And one day it's, 'Oh! You are still alive?'"

Dad passed away when Charles was barely two years old. Charles didn't get to know his grandfather in person, but he got to know him through me.

For nineteen years, I have been celebrating my son's birthday with our entire family—easily twenty of us. It is no longer in my childhood home, my parents are no longer there, but we still eat at the same table where I announced his arrival, the same table where my mother laid the dishes to celebrate my birthdays.

Nineteen years ago, I couldn't imagine someone calling me Mom, and nineteen years later I can't imagine not having someone around who calls me Mom.

The love I was given all my life has reached another level, a certain magic—my egregore!

PENNY FOR YOUR THOUGHTS

Do you or your family have a motto, a saying you often repeat? What makes you look at the people around you and think "I love this person"? When was the last time you felt like a warrior?

What is your egregore made of?

EPILOGUE

GOOD VIBES ONLY

Everything in life is vibration.

—ALBERT EINSTEIN

PLAYLIST

Look for the Good · JASON MRAZ
Le bonheur · CORNEILLE
C'est la vie · COLLECTIF MÉTISSÉ
Levitating · DUA LIPA AND DABABY
Shoop · SALT-N-PEPA
Titanium · DAVID GUETTA AND SIA
Good Vibrations · MARKY MARK AND THE FUNKY BUNCH
Il est où le bonheur · CHRISTOPHE MAÉ
Hymn for the Weekend · COLDPLAY
Let's Groove · EARTH, WIND & FIRE
Born to Be Alive · PATRICK HERNANDEZ
Celebration · KOOL & THE GANG
Sexual Healing · MARVIN GAYE
Live is Life · OPUS
Gettin' Jiggy Wit It · WILL SMITH
Je joue de la musique · CALOGERO
Good Vibrations · THE BEACH BOYS
Danza Kuduro · DON OMAR
High on Life · MARTIN GARRIX AND BONN
Tatouage · PIERRE LAPOINTE
Lovely Day · BILL WITHERS
Je te laisserai des mots · PATRICK WATSON
All You Need Is Love · THE BEATLES

SURFING THE SAME VIBE

June 2020. My husband and I were invited to a lobster party on our street. It was a tradition. Every year in June, our neighbour JF invites a group of fun people, a mix of friends and neighbours. It was perfect because we didn't have far to go! We all pitched in, but JF took care of cooking the lobsters. He is an amazing host. The rest of us took care of salads, hors d'oeuvres, and desserts.

That year, the food was great and so was the conversation. We were introduced to a new couple who arrived a little later, Isa and Pat. They were funny and easy-going. They travelled a lot around the world. Pat works for his family's business, making guitars and selling them around the world—even Sting has one! Isa is a lot like me. She loves good food, and we have lots in common. We clicked! So much so that we sat and talked until past two in the morning.

We promised to see each other soon, which we did, since we lived one minute away from each other. Thank God, because with Covid hitting, we did not get to see many friends. Most of my friends are old friends from my childhood and adolescence. As we get older, we are so caught up with our routine—work, family, responsibilities… It leaves very little time to see existing friends and even less to make new ones. When we meet someone new, there is no guarantee we will connect. Needless to say, I experienced a "friend crush" like the ones I used to feel in childhood. The feeling was mutual. I wanted to know everything about my new friends. We seemed to have the same values, liked the same Netflix shows, loved good food and desserts and spending Saturday nights with friends!

Isa's birthday was coming up, and I wanted to get her a gift, but I still felt I knew very little about her. So I stopped by her house, had a glass of wine, and asked her tons of questions, just like kids do. Too bad we rarely do that as adults because it's fun! I asked her favourite colour, favourite movie, favourite everything… We laughed. I smiled all the way back home.

It got me thinking: When was the last time I had such a conversation with my old friends? What was their favourite colour? Their favourite movie? As I dug a little more into my thoughts, I started asking different questions: Why do I connect with certain people and not with others? Why are there people I've been friends with since I was five and others I feel no attachment to or lost track of without ever thinking about it twice? My theory is that it has to do with something stronger than just having things in common. Of course, that is very important—having the same family and social values, speaking the same language, liking the same things—but I think there is something deeper that happens in the subconscious, something more complicated.

I do not have all the answers, far from it, but I think that a big part of it is about riding the same vibe. I am always attracted to good vibes. We cannot be in a happy mood 365 days a year, 24/7. I am well aware that life will throw challenges and obstacles my way, but I choose to look beyond and further. Just like in the shows of my childhood, I keep thinking everything will turn out okay in the end.

I remember working as a publicist for a rock star. I was accompanying him for a media tour. We were having lunch before his next interview. He was all dressed in black: black leather jacket, black pants, black belt, black t-shirt... Even his voice and his songs were dark. He was telling me that he was looking for a new apartment. He was looking for something that didn't have a lot of light. He went on and on about how people who loved light bugged the heck out of him. He needed darkness to sleep, to write, to live. "How could anybody like light?" he said while I listened. He complained during the whole lunch hour. I looked at my watch—saved by the bell! It was time to head to the next interview. I figured it was better not to let him know that the kind of person who loved bright apartments with lots of light was sitting right in front of him. Nope, we do not all ride the same vibe! For that reason, we might not be able to connect with everybody around us in the same way, or as deeply, or for as long.

It's as if each one of us saw life differently depending on the glasses we wear. Some wear very dark glasses so they see darkness pretty much everywhere. Others wear rose-tinted glasses, so they tend to see life in a more positive light.

We need both the darkness and the light. One makes us appreciate the other. We need sunny days and rainy days, or nature will not survive. We need opposites. Sometimes a tall person will need a short person, and a short person will need a tall one. We all need each other.

PURPOSE TO GET TO THE MAGIC

I think life is about purpose and magic. Everyone has a purpose. In professional American football, you need a good coach, captain, good offence, defence, quarterback, linemen, running backs… Same thing in hockey. It does not matter how great your goaltender is, he cannot make it alone; he needs his team. If you want to build a house, you will need an architect, a contractor, a material provider, a designer, a plumber, an electrician—a whole crew! Suppose you want to make a hit movie like *Star Wars, Dune, Avatar,* or *C.R.A.Z.Y.* In that case, you will need a great director but also great actors, great music, great costume designers, great editors, and so many more people in the background you will never hear about but who play an essential part. Just watch acceptance speeches at the Oscars and see how many people thank their wife, family, teachers, and the people they met along the way.

Life is exactly the same. It is made of great elements, but its magic lies in its people and the energy around them. We rarely talk about energy or the element of magic in our lives. We leave it to the spiritual world. But if a brilliant man, a scientist like Einstein, acknowledged seventy years ago that everything is vibration, why can't we? Isn't it all around us?

Tiger Woods almost always wears a red shirt for the final round of a tournament, a superstition that comes from his mother who believes red represents power. Michael Jordan, the best basketball player ever, would always wear his UNC shorts under his NBA shorts for luck. Serena Williams does not change her socks once during a tournament. Wade Boggs, famous baseball player for the Red Sox and the Yankees, would draw the word "Chai" in the dirt (Hebrew for "life") before coming up for bats. The famous lucky beard of Björn Borg, the great tennis player of the eighties, is one of sports history's most famous superstitions.

One of the greatest hockey goaltenders in the history of the NHL, Patrick Roy, was a firm believer in the power of superstition. The former Montreal Canadien would skate backwards towards the net and turn around at the last second, an act he believed made the net shrink. During the game, he would talk to the goal posts, thanking them when a puck was deflected and often touching them. This almost spiritual relationship with his goal earned him the nickname St. Patrick and an unprecedented three Conn Smythe trophies. Each one of these professional athletes uses material items that represent luck to them, so they can be reminded of the good vibe from one game to another. Superstition or luck?

MY LIFE MOTTO: GOOD VIBES ONLY

I was too young to be a hippie, but it was all around me. On TV, in movies, on the radio, in fashion, in the yellow and orange colours everywhere, in the decorations around me...

I grew up with *Bewitched*, *I Dream of Jeannie*, *The Flying Nun*, and reruns of *Father Knows Best*. These TV shows all told us that life was not perfect, but in the end, all ends well!

In the eighties, I was still watching TV. I dreamed of dancing in class like they did in *Fame*, being strong like Wonder Woman, being part of a big perfect family like in

Eight Is Enough and *The Cosby Show*, taking *The Love Boat* to find my next boyfriend, and flying to *Fantasy Island* to make all my wishes come true. In later years, I relaxed on my couch, pretending I was hanging out and laughing with my friends from *Cheers*, *Seinfeld*, and *Friends*.

Deep down inside, I knew life was different; I could make the distinction between life and television. Today with all the reality shows, TV can very well be confused with real life.

I am a story addict. So, to this day, I watch TV every week, except that instead of watching just one show I can now watch a whole season without any ads! Very dangerous! I watch so many different things. *Game of Thrones*, *Peaky Blinders*, *Last Kingdom*, *Sex Education*... It is a far cry from *Friends*! It's like reality did a 360 on television: violence, sex, no rules, no limits, no boundaries! Sometimes boundaries are good. If you never give a child boundaries, good luck going through adolescence with him in the house!

WHEN THE GOOD VIBES GET LOST

We spend so much time on the fast lane of the highway of life, running at a crazy speed on a never-ending wheel, losing all control. We are so bombarded by ads, shows, ideas, that we become numb, and in order to come back to life, we need an electric shock. Sometimes it is a trip to the hospital, sometimes it is the whole world stopping, all at the same time.

What if the pandemic happened in order to open our eyes? Make us stop and think? Leave the fast lane of the highway and drive on the slow country road to admire the scenery, admire what we have been missing—nature, people, good times, lessons, and *ourselves*?

I have always asked myself lots of questions. I have always been curious. It's in my nature. But getting older and going through a pandemic, I started listening more and looking around, asking myself: Who am I? Why am I this way? How can I stay on solid ground while everything around looks like it is collapsing? It got me back to my motto, "Good vibes only."

We often hear that before stepping into the future, we should know our past. It is one thing to know your past, but having a deep understanding of it is another.

To love others, you need to love yourself. To love yourself, you need to know yourself.

I believe that I grow and evolve every day (at least I hope I do!). Maybe it was the influence of my eldest sister's generation and the hippies I saw in the news, pop culture, and in her friends who came over? The keywords seemed to be all about peace and love. I find good vibrations are really about the "love vibration." It sounds spiritual, but it is much simpler than that.

"Good vibes only" does not mean you ignore how you feel. It just means you are aware of it, and you move on. "Good vibes only" means being grounded, and being grounded means being connected—connected to who you are and to those around you. Sometimes, to get there, you need to take the country road and look in the rear-view mirror. You need to understand the road you have travelled to understand the road ahead. Maybe along the way you'll meet a hitchhiking hippie, and you can exchange great stories about things that you are both grateful for, realizing how much they helped you grow.

To me, "good vibes only" means that I have to have gratitude for everything that worked out and did not work out in my life, saying thank you to everybody who helped me along the way in a big or small way.

You need that good vibration in the mix. You can have all the training and knowledge in sports, business, or life, but to win, you need that special energy, that chemistry, that vibe that solidifies it all. The vibe that says, "Yes we can!" and lifts you up to a higher level.

When I stop and think, I realize that the most memorable moments in my life have nothing to do with money, luxury, or medals. Instead, they have everything to do with a pure moment of love between two people in a car, in a home, or around a table, pure moments I did not expect or plan. It's those moments, those mini egregores, that we usually don't pay attention to but end up being engraved into our memory.

I realize to what extent so many people have impacted my life by their actions, their beliefs, and maybe even their dreams and their thoughts.

I hope this book helps you realize the many stories around you that helped you be who you are. I hope you get to know yourself a little more. I hope you feel gratitude. I hope it helps you connect more with yourself and with others. I hope you see the energy, the life force that helps you be you.

As I get older, it becomes clear to me that we cannot reach happiness on our own. It takes a village, a community of people, working together on a same good vibe, a good energy, a love energy, like a strong, positive egregore. The Beatles sing "All You Need Is Love," and that is what I wish for you. I wish you love.

PENNY FOR YOUR THOUGHTS

What's your story? What has influenced it? What is your motto? What were your favourite TV shows as you were growing up? Do you find links between shows you liked, your generation, and your essence? What do you need in order to experience good vibes? What characteristics do all your friends have in common?

When was the last time you felt an egregore, a time you were connecting strongly with one person or a group (family, friends, colleagues…) to reach a common goal (happiness, well-being, success)?

Whatever happens in your life, don't judge the next guy. Ask him about his story. In a divided world, let's make an effort to build communities and uplift each other.

RECIPES

The secret ingredient is always love.

—ANONYMOUS

PLAYLIST

Watermelon Sugar · HARRY STYLES
Passionfruit · DRAKE
American Pie · DON MCLEAN
Ice Cream · SARAH MCLACHLAN
Coconut · HARRY NILSSON
That's Amore · DEAN MARTIN
Sugar · MAROON 5
Banana Pancakes · JACK JOHNSON
Vegetables · THE BEACH BOYS
C is for Cookie · COOKIE MONSTER
Gravy · DEE DEE SHARP
Salade de fruits · BOURVIL
Strawberry Fields Forever · THE BEATLES
Eat it · WEIRD AL YANKOVIC
Sugar Sugar · THE ARCHIES
Dessert · DAWIN
I Can't Help Myself · FOUR TOPS
Les fraises et les framboises · LA FAMILLE SOUCY
Le pouding à l'Arsenic · LES COLOCS
La cuisinière · LA BOTTINE SOURIANTE

This book would not be complete if I didn't leave you with a taste of my childhood. Some of these recipes might be familiar to my fellow Quebeckers. Good food is what brings us together and creates the best memories. I invite you to create great memories of your own by discovering the tastes and the smells of my childhood. Bon appétit!

ASPIC

Aspic was a very popular recipe in Quebec when I was a child. It is a savory jelly made from meat broth. Ingredients may include meat, poultry, fish, eggs, vegetables, but I prefer the ones with fruits!

Historically, meat-based jelly was invented before fruit or vegetable jellies. The first known aspic recipe dates back to the end of the fourteenth century. In the eighteenth century, Marie-Antoine Carême, a French chef, created the *chaudfroid* ("hot-cold" in French), whose name refers to its method of preparation: cooked hot, served cold. Aspic was used as a *chaudfroid* sauce, with preparations based on fish or poultry. Adding flavor, it also kept cooked meat fresh and isolated from air and bacteria. Aspic made its way to North America in the early twentieth century, becoming extremely popular in the 1950s.

Here is a recipe for my favourite aspic Mom used to make, *l'aspic délicieuse*.

Ingredients:
- 2/3 teaspoon of lemon jelly
- 1/4 teaspoon of salt
- 1 teaspoon of grated carrots
- 1/4 teaspoon of uncoated apples
- 1 tablespoon of boiling water
- 1 tablespoon of pineapple juice
- 1/4 teaspoon of chopped pineapple
- 1/3 teaspoon of sweet pickles, diced
- 2 teaspoons of vinegar

Preparation:
- Heat the juice with water; add salt and vinegar.
- Cool in iced water.
- When the mixture has almost taken, incorporate fruits and vegetables.
- Pour into individual molds rinsed with cold water. Let it take.
- Unmold on the lettuce.

MARSHMALLOW BITES

This was the dessert Dad made after we had left home. He used to cook it every time he wanted us to come visit. It became my favourite dessert.

Ingredients:
- 1/3 cup of butter at room temperature
- 1 cup of brown sugar
- 1 egg
- 5 ml of vanilla extract
- 3/4 cup of all-purpose flour
- 1 teaspoon of baking powder
- 1/4 teaspoon of salt
- 1/2 cup of chopped walnuts
- 2 cups of miniature plain marshmallows

Ingredients for the icing:
- 1/2 cup of butter
- 1 cup of brown sugar
- 1/4 cup of warm milk
- 1/4 cup of icing and sieved sugar

Preparation:
- Preheat the oven to 350°F, grease an 8-inch square pyrex mold.
- Mix the butter and brown sugar with an electric blender for 3 minutes. Add the egg and vanilla extract. Mix for another 2 minutes.
- Using a rubber spatula, incorporate flour, baking powder, salt, and walnuts.
- Pour the mixture into the greased mold. Make sure the surface is even. Bake for about 25 minutes.
- Once baked, place the miniature marshmallows on the hot crust. Put back in the oven for about 2 minutes.
- Take out of the oven, and set aside while you prepare the icing.

Preparation for the frosting:
- In a small saucepan, melt the butter over medium heat. Add the brown sugar and bring to a boil by stirring constantly.

- Once it boils, simmer gently for 2 minutes while stirring. Remove from heat and add the milk.
- Put back on the stove and bring back to full boiling. Turn the heat off and let cool for 10 minutes.
- Add the icing sugar and mix well with the wooden spoon.
- Cover on the marshmallows and spread well.
- Leave for 1 hour at room temperature, cut and enjoy with a glass of milk.

EMPTY FRIDGE VEGETABLE SOUP

8–10 servings

Ingredients:
- vegetable oil, for cooking
- 1 yellow onion, finely chopped
- 1 cup of fresh parsley
- salt (Herbamare) and pepper, to taste
- 4 cloves of garlic, finely chopped
- 2 teaspoons of spices of your choice (turmeric, cardamom, cumin, etc.)
- 8 cups of vegetables of your choice, sliced or cut into quarters (carrot, potato, celery, etc.)
- 8 cups of chicken broth
- fresh herbs of your choice, for serving

Preparation:
- In a pot, heat the vegetable oil and cook the onion for 8 minutes or until soft. Season.
- Add the garlic and spices and cook for 2 more minutes.
- Add the vegetables to the broth. Season and let simmer for 20 minutes or until the vegetables are cooked. Adjust the seasoning if necessary and serve topped with fresh herbs.
- Decorate with parsley.

CHOMEUR'S PUDDING

Chomeur's pudding literally translates as "the unemployed man's pudding" and is also known as the "the poor man's pudding." This dessert originated in Quebec in the Great Depression. Legend says that Georgette Falardeau, the wife of Montreal's mayor Camillien Houde, invented this treat to allow the wives of workers to comfort their husbands affected by the layoffs with a good dose of brown sugar, hence its name.

This dessert became popular in 1950s Quebec, and my nanny Madame Nadon used to make the best chomeur's pudding.

8 servings

Ingredients:
- 1 1/2 cups of all-purpose flour
- 1 teaspoon of baking powder
- 1 egg
- 1 cup of white sugar
- 1/4 cup of margarine
- 1 cup of milk
- 2 cups of water
- 2 cups of brown sugar
- 1/4 cup of margarine
- 1/4 teaspoon of vanilla extract

Preparation:
- Preheat the oven to 325°F. Grease a 9x13-inch baking dish.
- Sift the flour and baking powder together in a small bowl. Beat the egg, sugar, and 1/4 cup of margarine together in a large bowl. Add the flour mixture alternately with the milk to the egg mixture, stirring just to combine. Pour the batter into the prepared dish.
- Bring the water to a boil in a saucepan; stir the brown sugar, 1/4 cup of margarine, and vanilla extract into the water, and return to a boil for 2 minutes. Pour the sauce over the batter.
- Bake in the preheated oven until the centre is set, about 45 minutes.

BECHAMEL

4 servings

Ingredients:
- 4 tablespoon of butter
- 2 cups of milk
- 4 tablespoon of plain, all-purpose flour
- salt and pepper

Preparation:
- Chop the butter into cubes, about the size of dice.
- Pour the milk into a heavy-bottomed pan, and add the butter and flour.
- Place the pan over a medium heat, and stir constantly with a balloon whisk.
- As the milk becomes hot, the butter starts to melt and will absorb the flour.
- Keep stirring, and you will feel the mixture change. Once it starts to thicken, use a small wooden spoon to stir the sauce, ensuring you get to the very edges of the pan.
- Reduce the heat to the lowest setting. and let the sauce cook gently for 5 minutes, stirring from time to time.
- Remove the pan from the heat, and check your sauce for seasoning.
- Enjoy on pasta, chicken, or broccoli.

BEEF BOURGUIGNON

6 servings

Ingredients:
- 6 slices of bacon, cut into lardons
- 3 1/2 tablespoons of extra-virgin olive oil
- 3 pounds of stewing beef, cut into 2-inch chunks
- 1 large carrot, sliced
- 1 large white onion, sliced
- 1 pinch of coarse salt and freshly ground pepper
- 2 tablespoons of all-purpose flour
- 3 cups of red wine, like a Pinot Noir or Merlot
- 2 1/2 to 3 1/2 cups of beef stock
- 1 tablespoon of tomato paste
- 3 cloves of smashed garlic
- 1/2 teaspoon of thyme
- 1 crumbled bay leaf
- 18 to 24 small pearl onions
- 3 1/2 tablespoons of butter
- 1 herb bouquet (4 sprigs parsley, 2 sprigs thyme, 1 bay leaf)
- 1 pound of fresh white mushrooms, quartered
- 2 tablespoon of fresh cut parsley

Preparation:
- Simmer bacon lardons in 4 cups of water for 10 minutes. (Lardon is the French culinary term referring to thin strips of bacon, cut approximately 1/4-inch thick.) Drain and pat dry.
- Preheat oven to 450°F. In a large Dutch oven (Creuset type), sauté the bacon in 1 tablespoon of oil for about 3 minutes, until it starts to lightly brown. Remove with a slotted spoon and set aside.
- Dry the beef with a few paper towels for better browning. In batches, sear the beef on all sides in the Dutch oven. Set aside with the bacon.
- Back in the pot, add the sliced carrots and onions; sauté in fat until browned, about 3 minutes. If there's any excess fat, drain it now.
- Add the bacon and beef back to the pot. Season with 1/2 teaspoon coarse salt and 1/4 teaspoon ground pepper. Toss. Sprinkle with flour

and toss once more. Place in the centre of the oven for 4 minutes.

- Remove pot from oven; toss beef and place back in the oven for 4 more minutes. Remove the pot from the oven and reduce the heat to 325°F.
- To the pot, add the wine and stock. The liquid should barely cover the meat and vegetables. Add the tomato paste, garlic, and thyme. Bring to a light simmer on the stove, then cover and simmer in the lower part of the oven for 3 to 4 hours, or until the meat is easily pierced.
- In the last hour of cooking, bring 1 1/2 tablespoons of butter and 2 teaspoons of oil to a medium heat in a sauté pan. Add the pearl onions, and toss around in the fat until they've browned, 10 minutes. Then stir in 1/2 cup of beef stock, a small pinch of salt and pepper and the herb bouquet. Reduce the heat to low, and simmer the onions for about 40 minutes, until the liquid has evaporated, and the onions are tender.
- Remove the onions, and set aside. Discard the herb bouquet, and wipe out the skillet. Add the remaining butter and oil, and bring to a medium heat.
- Add the mushrooms, and cook for about 5 minutes, shaking the pan to coat with the butter.
- Place a colander over a large pot. Drain the beef stew through the colander and into the pot. Place the pot with the sauce over a medium heat, and simmer for about 5 minutes, skimming any fat on top. Pour the beef and vegetables back into the Dutch oven. Add the pearl onions and mushrooms to the pot. Pour the sauce over the beef mix, and simmer an additional 3 to 5 minutes.

BAKED BEANS

This is my dad's favourite.

12 servings

Ingredients:
- 8 cups of water
- 1 pound of dry navy beans, rinsed and picked through
- 1 tablespoon of olive oil
- 6 ounces of salt pork, diced
- 6 ounces of bacon, cut into small pieces
- 1 small onion, minced
- 1 1/2 cups of water, divided
- 1/4 cup of ketchup
- 1/3 cup of molasses
- 1/4 cup of brown sugar
- 1 tablespoon of yellow mustard

Preparation:
- Combine water and beans in a multi-functional pressure cooker. Close and lock the lid. Select high pressure; set timer for 15 minutes. Allow 10 to 15 minutes for pressure to build.
- Release pressure for 20 minutes. Unlock and remove the lid. Drain and rinse the beans with cold water, and set aside. Rinse and wipe out pressure cooker, and place back into the pressure cooker.
- Turn on pressure cooker, and select the Saute function. Heat olive oil until shimmering, 2 to 3 minutes. Add salt pork, bacon, and onion, and briefly cook until fat begins to render, 1 to 2 minutes. Pour in 1/2 cup of water, and scrape any brown bits off the bottom. Turn pressure cooker off.
- Whisk together ketchup, molasses, brown sugar, mustard, and remaining 1 cup of water in a small bowl. Return cooked beans to the pot along with the ketchup mixture. Gently stir to combine. Close and lock the lid. Select high pressure; set timer for 35 minutes. Allow 10 to 15 minutes for pressure to build.
- Release pressure for 20 minutes. Unlock and remove the lid. Beans will thicken upon cooling. Serve immediately or freeze portions for later.

CRETONS

12 servings

Ingredients:
- 1 pound of ground pork
- 1 cup of milk
- 1 onion, chopped
- chopped garlic
- salt and pepper, to taste
- 1 pinch of ground cloves
- 1 pinch of ground allspice
- 1/4 cup of dry bread crumbs

Preparation:
- Place the ground pork, milk, onion, and garlic into a large saucepan. Season with salt, pepper, cloves, and allspice.
- Cook over medium heat for about 1 hour, then stir in the bread crumbs.
- Cook for 10 more minutes. Adjust seasonings to taste. Transfer to a small container and keep refrigerated.
- Serve on toast with sweet onion mustard. Perfect with eggs in the morning.

FRENCH TOAST

4 servings

Ingredients:
- 1 teaspoon of ground cinnamon
- 1/4 teaspoon of ground nutmeg
- 2 tablespoons of sugar
- 4 tablespoons of butter
- 4 eggs
- 1/4 cup of milk
- 1/2 teaspoon of vanilla extract
- 8 slices of challah, brioche, or white bread
- 1/2 cup of maple syrup, warmed

Preparation:
- In a small bowl, combine cinnamon, nutmeg, and sugar, and set aside briefly.
- In a 10-inch or 12-inch skillet, melt butter over medium heat. Whisk together cinnamon mixture, eggs, milk, and vanilla, and pour into a shallow container such as a pie plate.
- Dip bread in egg mixture. Fry slices until golden brown, then flip to cook the other side. Serve with syrup and warm berries.

BASIC FRENCH VINAIGRETTE

Makes about 1/2 cup

Ingredients:
- 2 tablespoons of finely chopped shallots
- 2 tablespoons of red- or white-wine vinegar
- 1/4 teaspoon of fine sea salt, or to taste
- 2 teaspoons of Dijon mustard
- 4 to 6 tablespoons of extra-virgin olive oil
- chopped garlic
- freshly ground black pepper, to taste

Preparation:
- In a small bowl, whisk together the shallots, vinegar, and 1/4 teaspoon of fine sea salt. Let the mixture stand for 10 minutes.
- Whisk in the mustard, then add the oil in a very slow, thin, steady stream, whisking constantly until the dressing is emulsified. Season with fine sea salt and freshly ground black pepper.
- The vinaigrette can be prepared ahead and refrigerated, in an airtight container, up to 1 week.

TAGLIATELLE WITH MUSHROOM ESCARGOT CREAM SAUCE

4 servings

Ingredients:
- 2 cups of dried wild mushrooms, rinsed well and soaked in warm water for 30 minutes
- 1 small shallot, minced
- 1 garlic clove, minced
- 2 tablespoons of butter, divided
- 1 cup of heavy cooking cream
- 1 cup of frozen or drained canned peas
- 1 can of escargots, drained
- 1 teaspoon of dried tarragon
- salt and pepper to taste
- 1 tablespoon of chopped fresh parsley
- enough cooked tagliatelle for 4 servings

Preparation:
- Drain the mushrooms, and roughly chop.
- In a saucepan, heat 1 tablespoon of butter, and saute garlic and shallot until fragrant.
- Add cream and mushrooms, and if using frozen peas, add them now too.
- Simmer for several minutes until cream begins to thicken.
- Stir in tarragon, parsley, and drained snails, and if using canned peas now is the time to add.
- Add the remaining tablespoon of butter and stir to heat through.
- Serve over pasta.

ROAST BEEF

4 servings

Ingredients:
- a 2-pound roast of beef, barded and bound with string
- 1 cup of Dijon mustard
- 2 cloves of garlic
- 2 teaspoons of olive oil
- 1 sprig of fresh thyme, or 1/4 teaspoon of dried thyme
- salt and freshly ground black pepper

Preparation:
- Preheat the oven to 450°F.
- Cover the beef with mustard.
- Peel the garlic cloves, cut it in half lengthwise, and slice the halves into slivers.
- Insert the point of a sharp knife into the roast, remove, and insert a garlic sliver. Repeat all around the roast until you have used up the garlic.
- Spread half the olive oil around the bottom and sides of your roasting pan, the other half around the meat. Sprinkle with thyme leaves.
- Place the beef in the oiled pan, turn the oven down to 425°F, and roast for 25 minutes for very rare meat, 30 minutes for medium rare, 35 minutes for medium. Allow to rest for a few minutes after removing from the oven.

MASHED POTATOES

Ingredients:
- 1 teaspoon of garlic powder
- 4 pounds of russet potatoes
- 1/4 teaspoon of black pepper
- 1 1/2 teaspoon of salt
- 6 tablespoons of salted butter
- 1 1/2 cups of warm whole milk
- 1 uncooked chopped white onion
- 1 teaspoon of garlic
- a touch of cream (optional)

Preparation:
- Heat the potatoes. Mash them. Add milk, butter, garlic, salt, and onion. Mix. Taste, and add a touch of cream if needed.

Acknowledgements

There is a world between having the idea of a book and holding the book in your hand. I could not have done it by myself. It takes a village. I wish to thank all these incredible people that stuck by me. Some are part of my family, some are good friends, and some are precious collaborators. Thank you to everybody who believed in me and helped me in some way or another to make this book a reality. Sometimes by your encouraging words, sometimes by pushing through with me, sometimes by just crossing my path.

Thanks to Martin, Charles, Carole, Josée, Alexa, Lynn Thériault, Annick Laplante, Mélanie, Catherine Bridgman, Zackary, Caro, Marc-Henri, Hans, Roxane Tremblay, Yolande Guy, Huguette Guy, Sylvie L'Archevêque, Alexis, Adrienne, Marisa Bove, Erik, Dahna W., Anne-Marie Salloum, Nathalie Pelletier, Nathalie Colpron, PK, Stéphanie Bock, Marie-Jo, Cath, Soph, Paul, Nick, Patrick Godin, Isabelle Molleur, Maggie A., Steven Vandal, Liane Bertrand, Marc, Sylvie, Hadrien, Florence, Manon Thériault, Laur, Laurie Loo, Lyda Mclallen, and Paul Neuviale.

And of course, I would like to thank my mom and dad. Without their loving presence, you would not be reading this!

ABOUT THE AUTHOR

Elizabeth Péladeau is a public relations coach and author. Ever since she was a little girl, Elizabeth was always inspired by people's stories. This has led her to an accomplished career in communications in which she uses her knack for capturing the essence of her clients and making them shine. During the pandemic, she started looking at the puzzle that is her own life story in order to uplift those around her. The picture that emerged is captured in this book. Elizabeth lives in Montreal with her husband and son.

⊙ lizlionzest

CPSIA information can be obtained
at www.ICGtesting.com
Printed in the USA
LVHW011812180322
713801LV00006B/466